Criminal
Justice

SAGE COURSE COMPANIONS
KNOWLEDGE AND SKILLS *for* SUCCESS

Criminal Justice

Ursula Smartt

 SAGE Publications

London • Thousand Oaks • New Delhi

First published 2006

 SAGE Publications Ltd
1 Oliver's Yard
55 City Road
London EC1Y 1SP

SAGE Publications Inc.
2455 Teller Road
Thousand Oaks, California 91320

SAGE Publications India Pvt Ltd
B-42, Panchsheel Enclave
Post Box 4109
New Delhi 110 017

British Library Cataloguing in Publication data

A catalogue record for this book is available from the British Library

ISBN-10 1 4129 0706 3   ISBN-13 978-1-4129-0706-4
ISBN-10 1 4129 0707 1 (pbk)   ISBN-13 978-1-4129-0707-1 (pbk)

Library of Congress Control Number: 2005931543

Typeset by C&M Digitals (P) Ltd., Chennai, India
Printed on paper from sustainable resources
Printed and bound in Great Britain by Cromwell Press Ltd, Trowbridge, Wiltshire

<table>
<tr><td></td><td></td></tr>
</table>

contents

part one
introduction

1.1

introduction to your course companion

Welcome to the *Sage Course Companion: Criminal Justice*. I hope you will enjoy this companion on Criminal Justice and that it will enhance your interest in the criminal justice system. This book is intended to provide you with two things: firstly, a quick introduction to the subject matter and what studying for Criminal Justice is all about, secondly as a revision and quick reference guide to the main issues in contemporary Criminal Justice and the study of Criminology.

This book isn't intended to replace your set textbooks or lectures, it is here to save you time when you are revising for your exams or preparing assessed coursework. Note that RE-vision implies that you have already looked at the subject the first time round! It is hoped that this course companion will give you the necessary skills by using the **Tips!** features to show you the key areas you will need to study. Additionally, **Common pitfalls** will show you what not to do and give you some handy hints. These features will help you anticipate exam questions and provide guidelines on what your examiners are looking for. This book should be seen as a framework in which to organise your subject matter, and to extract the most important points from your textbooks, lecture notes, and other learning materials on your course.

You will also be directed to **Key thinkers** in the field. This course companion has been built around the main textbooks in Criminal Justice and Criminology, summarised at the end of each section in Part 2, and in the bibliography at the end of the book, together with useful Internet sources for further research. It is obvious that in this area of study there is a vast amount of literature available; this book provides guidance on the most familiar ones.

Part 3 focuses on various study skills and will help you learn more efficiently in the Criminal Justice domain. Learning is best accomplished by seeing the information from several different angles – which is why you attend lectures and tutorials, read textbooks, and read around the subject in general. This book will help you to bring together all kinds of different sources.

The purpose of this course companion is to be an *addition to* (not instead of) your course books. It is intended as a means of memorising content and familiarising yourself with the basics of Criminal Justice; to help you prepare for your exams; and to plan and construct assessed essays. Additional research is suggested in the **Taking it further** sections for those students who wish to improve their performance and achieve excellent grades. The *Sage Course Companion: Criminal Justice* will help you structure and organise your thoughts, and enable you to get the most from your course and textbooks.

1.2	
how to use this book	

This book provides you with an easy-to-navigate guide to the commonly taught Criminal Justice and Criminology curriculum. The course companion presents you with ways of thinking and writing that examiners will be looking for when they start to grade and examine your work. This book should be used as a supplement to your textbook, set texts, lectures and seminar notes.

When is your course companion useful to you? If you are a new undergraduate Criminal Justice or Criminology student, you could buy the course companion at the beginning of the first semester (or term), and should find the guidance features useful throughout your undergraduate years of study (features such as: **Tips!** or **Common pitfalls**) since all core areas are covered. That said, the course companion is useful at any level of study (including postgraduate studies), also covering professional examinations (such as police, prison or probation service interviews or promotion exams). **Core areas** and **Running themes** (such as 'Human Rights') are provided in each section of Part 2, so that you can drop in on themes, and make connections.

You can use this book to give you a quick overview of the subject before you start studying Criminal Justice; in other words give yourself a brief preview of the course. It can then be used as a reference point throughout your degree, and as a revision aid for your exams. Each section contains the following features:

- Introduction to the topic – core areas of the curriculum
- Learning outcomes – what the examiner expects from you
- Running themes – the areas that will always be of interest to a Criminal Justice Specialist
- Tips! – on handling the information in exams, or reminders of key issues
- Common pitfalls – on what not to do or write
- Key thinkers – in the field; for useful quotes in exams or assessments
- Sample exam and assessment questions – with outlined answers and ideas for possible answers.

Part 1 continues to explain how to use this book, with a brief introduction to Criminal Justice and your academic life. Firstly, we want you to begin to think like a Criminal Justice Specialist: this means learning *how* to think academically. Examiners want to see that you can handle the basic concepts of the subject. In short, this means, well-constructed sentences; getting to the point immediately without much waffle; and correct referencing to legislation in the form of statutes (Acts of Parliament) or case law. You will also need to reference well and correctly. **Taking it further** will assist you to use learned source references correctly (e.g. books, journals etc), in order to develop your understanding further. If you are using the book for the first time, to give you an introduction to the subject, you will find Part 1 most useful.

Part 2 goes into the core curriculum in more detail, taking each topic and providing you with the key elements required; the ten sections will help you understand the workings of the Criminal Process of England and Wales. Remember: you will need to attend lectures and tutorial workshops and should not only use this course companion – you will need the deeper coverage provided by lectures and set texts.

What is most important for you as a Criminal Justice Specialist is to find the ability to communicate effectively in all aspects of your written and oral presentations. This text helps you develop these skills in order to become not only effective academically, but also in your professional life. You must therefore have good technical skills and be able to follow instructions well, which are implied in exam questions (e.g. 'discuss' or 'evaluate').

1.3	
navigation around the book	

Before you start your (revision) studies, you may wish to establish your principal sources of information, such as your course handbook, module study guide or workbook that accompany your course. Do you have sufficient primary source references, such as set textbooks, websites, course handouts and journal articles? You need to sort these supporting texts into **Running themes**; these are provided in Part 2 in connection with each topic area of the Criminal Justice curriculum. Make sure you are not working from old texts when working in a library. Check the copyright page of each book to establish the year of publication. Issues in Criminal Justice policy change constantly and have undergone vast changes over the past decade.

You should ensure that you have read the syllabus thoroughly and that you have a set of past exam papers and assessment questions at hand, so that you know which areas of the subject you are expected to study. Not all topic areas and themes in this book will be covered by your syllabus. Having obtained an overall impression of your targets of study (and Part 2 will give you these areas) you need to ask yourself the following questions:

- What areas do I understand?
- What areas do I not understand?

This book will then help you place emphasis on those areas of Criminal Justice which you find difficult by way of the **Tips!** features. A good way of revision is to firstly attend to a topic that you *do* understand which will leave you on a 'high' note. Then return to areas which cause you difficulty – this should be done on another day, and the **Common pitfalls** will help you avoid unnecessary mistakes. Then revisit your textbooks and additional course notes which you do not understand. This course companion will highlight the basic and fundamental principles in Criminal Justice and strip away detailed theory and analysis, often found in textbooks.

You can read this book in two ways:

1 **Skim-reading** (or speed-reading)

- Let your eyes skim the page (often referred to as 'diagonal reading')
- Make a note of the **Tips!** and use these as bullet points to memorise
- Look at the tables that summarise topic areas
- Use the **Core areas** of the curriculum section headings or the index to locate information
- Notice the **Running themes** sub-headings in Part 2.

2 **Slow and in-depth reading**

- Slow and careful reading of each part, and
- Additional reading of your textbooks
- Read with an inquiring mind and make critical notes as you read
- Take regular breaks during this kind of reading
- Make a note of all references in **Taking it further** (including/page/chapter numbers and headings in textbooks).

Read this Course Companion with a view towards:

- A basic understanding of Criminal Justice (to be expanded through your lectures, seminars, textbooks and further reading)
- Answering exam questions
- Preparing for an assignment
- Helping you concentrate and focus on concise answers
- Helping you think like a Criminal Justice Specialist (in the way the examiner wants you to).

Common exam and revision questions

At the end of each section in Part 2, you will be given some sample exam or assessment questions which are there to help you revise and to put pen to paper (exams are still handwritten!). You will also be provided with some suggested sample outline answers. Here is a general example:

Answering an exam question about crime and deviance

In order to answer such a question in an examination, the kinds of explanatory factors you may wish to use are fairly simple, even if measuring them is complex. Deviance factors include: social, psychological and biological facts about the offender (referred to as 'criminogenic'); economic, social and political aspects of the offence (for example, does the offence result in financial gain? Is it fun? Does it have a political aim?); the context within which the offender commits the offence (for example, does one need special skills or a particular social status to commit the offence?); and – most importantly – deeply held beliefs about human nature as described in the literature.

This is further expanded with plenty of examples in Part 3 (Study, writing and revision skills). Here is an example:

Preparing for an exam should always include:

- *Using past papers (including resit papers)*
- *Discussion about relevant issues raised in the exam question (use the **Running themes**)*
- *Distinguishing between facts and opinions about facts*
- *Taking account of factual information by using primary reference sources (never give your own opinion, unless it is substantiated).*

1.4	
introducing the features	

The key to success in your study of Criminal Justice is to learn how to think *academically* and like a Criminal Justice Specialist. In short, think theoretically and analytically. This course companion will advise you how to learn to speak the language of academic study required by the examiner, using the terms and phrases that mark out 'Criminal Justice speak' during the course of this book. Writing academically or giving an oral presentation on the subject means using a different style from everyday discourse.

Tips!

The **Tips** features (boxed and signalled by a tack), will help you structure and plan your answers. Planning your answers ensures that you have constructed a well-thought out exam or assessment essay. **Tips!** are all about passing an exam well, *how* to analyse data or how to present a critical argument. **Tips!** highlight key information and offer advice about applying the content of your lectures and textbooks to your studying. For example:

You will do well in an exam if:

- *You become aware of the many significant ways **Key thinkers** in Criminal Justice or Criminology have disagreed with one another quite fundamentally*
- *You point out to the examiner that Criminal Justice Specialists tend to reside in different camps in an often quite tribal fashion.*

Common pitfalls

The **Common pitfalls** features address your style of writing. They will help you avoid making common mistakes and point out negative factors in your answers.

For example:

Common pitfalls: Resist the temptation to start answering exam questions directly and immediately. Always read the question carefully, and make bullet-pointed notes before you start answering the question.

Learning outcomes

Your Criminal Justice course or Criminology module will most likely present you with 'learning outcomes'. These are usually mentioned at the beginning of your course handbook. **Learning outcomes** are elements of reflective practice in order to ensure successful student assessment and learning set by your university or college.

---

*Make a careful list of all the particular **Learning outcomes** on your course. No doubt, you will be tested on these in your exam. They summarise what your examiners expect from you in your assessment and exam answers. Make sure they are relevant to each topic area (e.g. the Magistrates' Courts).*

Key thinkers

Your course companion will point you to **Key thinkers** in Criminal Justice and Criminology. These are learned academics and most influential theorists in Criminal Justice or Criminology. They are worth citing in essays.

Taking it further

Each chapter concludes with a **Taking it further** section, designed to put the icing on the cake – i.e. give you the chance to write a top-class, 'distinction'-type essay. Additionally, it can help those students who wish to advance their knowledge and study in the field. The **Taking it further** sections are intended to show you how to appraise and analyse theory and advance your theoretical knowledge. Together with the **Key thinkers**, the selected bibliography and the useful websites in the appendices, students will be provided with the means to advance their Criminal Justice research and to become truly excellent scholars. **Taking it further** offers you a more critical and analytical approach and helps you produce work of outstanding quality. Here is an example:

Taking it **FURTHER**

If you wish to familiarise yourself with recent changes in Criminal Justice policy which has influenced legislation in sentencing and the new running of the criminal courts under the *Criminal Justice Act 2003* – you should know about Lord Justice Auld's *Review of the Criminal Courts, 2001.*

Textbook guide

This feature gives you guidance on the main textbooks you will be using on your course. These can be augmented via the bibliography and Internet sources list in Part 4.

Part 3 (Study, writing and revision skills) will give you additional guidance on how to study, including how to take notes, essay-writing skills and exam preparation. Grateful thanks go to David McIllroy who has kindly co-authored and innovated the template for this section.

I have customised his teaching and learning guide to the study of Criminal Justice and Criminology.

Additional resources

The **Bibliography** and **Internet sources and useful websites** assist you with additional reading and up-to-date sources. The **Glossary of Criminal Justice and legal terms** provides you with a kind of 'dictionary' to enhance your referencing. The **Chronology of crime events** gives you some topical information which might be useful to enhance your general knowledge in the area of study.

1.5	
criminal justice: a brief introduction	

The principal aim of this course companion is to give you the core curriculum 'in a nutshell' and to provide you with a broad outline of topic areas that may well come up in an exam or assessed component of your degree course. All the core areas are covered in the ten sections of Part 2, providing the essence of the various stages in the English criminal process. The order of sequence has been taken from an imaginary suspect's first arrest to his criminal conviction, sentence and punishment, providing an overview how the various Criminal Justice agencies 'process' a criminal.

The criminal justice system can be summarised by the following agencies:

- The Police Service
- The Crown Prosecution Service (CPS)
- The Court Service (Magistrates' and Crown Court)
- The National Probation Service (NPS)
- The Prison Service.

In November 2004, when Her Majesty The Queen opened Parliament, she outlined the Government's legislative programme for the forthcoming year with key legislation to reduce crime, anti-social behaviour and to combat re-offending (e.g. *Criminal Justice Act 2003*; *Anti-social Behaviour Act 2003*). New legislation was proposed to tackle persistent juvenile crime and anti-social behaviour through more effective rehabilitation and sentencing. The *Violent Crime Reduction Bill* was published on 8 June 2005; measures include making it illegal to manufacture or sell imitation firearms that could be mistaken for real firearms, and the introduction of Alcohol Disorder Zones (ADZs) which will require licensed premises to contribute to the cost of alcohol-related disorder in specific areas where it has been identified as a problem.

What, then, is the main purpose of a Criminal Justice System (CJS)? One of the main aims should be that the CJS of any country should deliver justice for all (also known as due process) whereby the criminally convicted are suitably punished ('just deserts' theory of punishment) and the convicted are assisted by the system (e.g. probation, restorative justice and prisons) to stop future offending and to lead a law-abiding life after their sentence has been served. Another main goal of the CJS today is to help victims of crime and to protect the innocent and vulnerable (e.g. children).

The CJS is also responsible for detecting crime and bringing it to justice – the major law enforcement agency being the police force. The purpose of the courts is to carry out court orders (e.g. collecting fines) and to sentence fairly without any prejudice. The Probation Service's main aims and objectives lie in the supervision of community sentences, presenting the courts with Pre-Sentence Reports (PSRs) and bringing back to court those who breach their community sentence with possible resulting in custodial punishment.

The CJS today is represented by a number of agencies and partners (voluntary organisations and private contractors). For the past decade, every Criminal Justice agency has been redesigned. One of these is the National Offender Management Service (NOMS) comprising prison and probation services. The British Crime Survey (BCS) has established that crime has been reduced by about 25% since 1999. Police statistics (recorded crime) show that the number of offences brought to justice has increased, however, police clear-up rates remain low and have resulted in a decrease in public confidence in the CJS. As stated above, there has been a wealth of Criminal Justice legislation over the past ten years, which has led to confusion and not necessarily a 'joined up' Criminal Justice System. The law has been reformed to make it fit for a modern

Criminal Justice System. The Government has introduced new coherent roles of the various agencies within the CJS which can be summarised under the following headings:

- National Criminal Justice Board
- 42 Local Criminal Justice Boards across England and Wales
- Office for Criminal Justice Reform.

The National Criminal Justice Board has presented a strategic plan with a vision of what the CJS will look like in 2008. This includes increasing public confidence in the CJS, giving victims and witnesses a consistently high standard of service, and rigorous enforcement and compliance with sentences and court orders. The 42 local CJS Boards are generally made of local chief officers of the police, the CPS, the NPS, HM Courts Service, YOTs and the Prison Service. Their main aims and objectives centre on:

- Improvement of local services to victims and witnesses
- Targeting persistent, prolific and potentially dangerous offenders
- Ensuring that the right charges are brought against offenders, and at the right time
- Increasing the number of court trials that proceed on the day they are listed
- Increasing the number of warrants that are enforced
- Ensuring that the local CJS gives high quality service
- Establishing what matters most to local people and to effectively engage with the local community, particularly black and minority ethnic communities and other minority groups.

Therefore, it is important for you to bear in mind that penal policies and thereafter Criminal Justice legislation are forever changing, influenced by public opinion, which, in turn, is greatly influenced by the mass media today. By the time this book goes to print, there may have already been further changes to Criminal Justice legislation.

By the end of Part 2, you should be aware of and have detailed knowledge of the various stages of the Criminal Justice process. Your course companion concentrates on both legal and criminological factors that shape the practical operation of the Criminal Justice process.

1.6

thinking like a criminal justice specialist

What do we mean by 'thinking like a Criminal Justice Specialist'? It means, thinking critically and writing academically in the style that is expected by your examiner on the Criminal Justice course. How can you begin to think and write like a Criminal Justice Specialist? You should be able to identify and use the terms and phrases that mark out academic and 'Criminal Justice' speak from that of everyday discourse and colloquialisms. You should recognise the impact of various disciplines and discourses within Criminal Justice and Criminology, such as Law, Sociology, Social Policy and Psychology.

If there is one aim that I would like to achieve with this book, it is that you become an 'all round student' who engages in and benefits from *all* the learning activities available to you, and that you should develop all the academic and personal skills that will put you in the driving seat to becoming a Criminal Justice Specialist. I hope this course companion will do just that.

It has been my specific objective that your *SAGE Course Companion: Criminal Justice* should motivate you and build up your confidence in studying for this subject. If you can recognise the value of these qualities, both across your academic programme and beyond graduation to the world of work, then I know I have achieved my main purpose. Hopefully, this book will serve you well in your continued academic study and a commitment to life-long learning. I have made every effort to keep this book up-to-date, the latest legislation being the *Criminal Justice Act 2003*, most of which came into force on 1 April 2005. To update your reading and knowledge in this field, use the recommended websites provided in Part 4.

Ursula Smartt
London 2006

part two
core areas of the curriculum

running themes in criminal justice

There are certain themes that will always be relevant to nearly every topic in Criminal Justice; we have called these **Running themes**. Below, you will find a list of all running themes in this course companion. These will then be touched on at the beginning of each of the ten sections in Part 2, and in the text (in bold print). It is important that you bear the themes in mind when answering questions in exams or assessments.

- **Human rights** – Impact on citizenship and civil rights (liberty; freedom of speech) and criminal procedure (right to a fair trial; freedom from torture etc.). The *Human Rights Act 1998* enshrined the European Convention on Human Rights and Fundamental Freedoms (1950) in UK law. The European Court of Human Rights sits in Strasbourg. The United Nations has set benchmarks by a series of human rights treaties that protect citizens across the world from human rights violations. These rights set legal precedents for each state. These include: racial discrimination; child abuse; human trafficking etc.
- **Inequality** – An imbalance between rich and poor. Sociologists found that a child's future is largely determined by social status rather than brains. Criminality is more likely in the 'haves' rather than the 'have-nots'. Deviant behaviour and crime are *not* the inherent properties of individuals but the results of a series of relationships, characteristic of a given society. Poverty, inequality and crime are part and parcel of any given society.
- **Fear of crime** – Many people in today's society express anxiety and fear about crime, and about being victimised. The following factors impact on public fear of crime levels: gender; age; past experiences with crime; where one lives; one's ethnicity etc. People react to fear in different ways. Some people try to avoid crime, others try to protect themselves from being victimised. The police forces have created numerous programmes to alleviate the fear of crime phenomenon, including Neighbourhood Watch and Crime Prevention schemes (Police Community Support Officers). The Government has implemented new legislation (e.g. *Crime and Disorder Act 1998*; *Criminal Justice Act 2003*) to tackle anti-social behaviour and persistent youth crime.
- **Victims of crime** (Victimology) – Refers to any person or group who has suffered injury or loss due to an illegal activity. The legal definition of 'victim' includes 'a person who has suffered direct, or threatened, physical, emotional or pecuniary harm as a result of the commission of a crime'. Group harms usually include hate crimes (e.g. racial). Victimology is a sub-field of Criminology and defines the

problem of crime. Victimologists use surveys of large numbers of people about the crimes that have been committed against them because official police statistics are known to be incomplete (dark figure). International data, derived from victimisation surveys are carried out each year by the US Department of Justice in the form of the National Crime Victimization Survey (NCVS) and the Home Office by means of the British Crime Survey (BCS) every two years. Victimologists estimate victimisation rates and risks and measure the true dimension of the problem. They also investigate how the Criminal Justice System handles the problem of crime (or not) and they examine societal responses to crime by looking at issues of human rights in line with proposed legislation.

- **Race** – Race is a process of social construction through the various means of socialisation, i.e. the family, school, church, peers and work friendships etc. Some hate crimes involve racial intimidation, ethnicity, religion, or other minority groups. Children are not born with a concept of race or their racial identity. Over a period of time, usually through school, they will label themselves and significant others by virtue of physically identifiable learned racial classifications. As this process is extended to those outside of the family, racial categorisation comes into being. Over time, we learn to differentiate between races as projected by significant social role models.

- **Gender** – Denotes a complex interplay of cultural and biological factors and is often confused with sex, which generally refers to biology and anatomy. You may have heard of 'gender bias', which refers to a set of qualities and behaviours expected from a female or male by society. Gender roles are learned and can be affected by factors such as education or economics. They vary widely within and among cultures. While an individual's sex does not change, gender roles are socially determined and can evolve over time. Gender roles and expectations are often identified as factors hindering the equal rights and status of women with adverse consequences that affect life, family, socioeconomic status and health. For this reason, gender, like sexuality, is an important element in crime and criminal statistics, and you may hear 'gender crime' and 'feminist criminology' that deals with the unequal position of women in the criminal courts. They argue that reasons for female criminality lie in social oppression and economic dependency on men and the state. Crimes committed by women are considered to be a final outward manifestation of an inner medical imbalance or social instability (e.g. shoplifting). Women generally commit less crime than men and are of a less violent nature. Their punishment appears to be aimed principally at treatment and resocialisation. Law enforcers often take the view that women are inferior and unstable because of their hormones and emotions, which makes them not easy to deal with. Criminality is often linked to women's unstable, irrational, neurotic and 'mad' behaviour.

- **Punishment** – A penalty for an offence. Society has punished its offenders over time with various means, from public torture (the stocks; hanging) in the middle ages, to prison in more recent times (19th century) and community punishment and rehabilitation from the mid-20th century onwards. Related words are 'penalty' and 'penology'. Each society creates different systems of punishment, which then shape the penal system (including prisons; probation;

law enforcement etc). Penology covers the application of clinical, managerial or social scientific methods or expertise to the disciplined study and evaluation of penal institutions. During Victorian times, young offenders were punished by being removed from the adult justice system (see Gladstone's, 1895 Report). Borstals were started in 1902, with the aim of turning young offenders into better citizens. Punishment by prison became more rehabilitative from the 1960s onwards whereby prisoners were given more meaningful work inside and 'prison industries' were introduced (e.g. HMP Coldingley, Surrey). Capital punishment was abolished in the UK in 1965. From the mid-1990s onwards, research showed that persistent young offenders were not growing out of crime. Over the past two decades, government legislation has become more punitive towards young offenders, and less rehabilitative, but more sympathetic towards victims of crime. With the introduction of Detention Centres in the early 1980s, the 'short, sharp shock' treatment for delinquent youths was pioneered. Electronic tagging began in the late 1990s, a form of home detention curfew punishment for offenders as a way of keeping them out of trouble or early release from prison (e.g. for burglars).

- **Globalisation** – of crime, this describes the evolution of crime as an organised criminal activity in the world, linked to consumerism and economic deprivation. Understanding the globalisation of crime means to examine the role that crime plays as an agent of social change, linked to, criminalisation, crime and social development, crime and social control, the political economy of crime, and crime in transitional cultures.

- **Criminalisation** – This describes the institutionalised process by which certain acts and behaviours are labelled as 'crimes' and against the law. It reflects the state's decision to regulate, control and punish selectively. Criminalisation is influenced by politics, public opinion and the media within the contexts of social class, gender, sexuality, race and age. It represents the technical and legal process by which certain unlawful acts are legislated against, and regulated through law enforcement (police; courts).

- **Crime and the media** – The media plays a substantial role in determining the amount of fear of crime that people hold. This comes from the fact that the media extensively and disproportionately covers crime stories. This leads people to believe that there is more crime than there actually is; believing that a great amount of crime exists in society leads people to fear.

No matter what topic area of the criminal process you are writing about or revising, it is not too difficult to predict that the same **Running themes** recur throughout the whole syllabus and will mark out your subject.

Always try to mention the **Running themes** in your essays. This shows the examiner how you have thought about the impact upon the topic studied and that you are aware of these recurring themes in Criminal Justice.

2.1

introduction to the criminal process of England and Wales

The main aim of this section is to promote greater understanding of the Criminal Justice System as a whole. You will learn to understand how the criminal law operates in practice by looking at the various agencies involved in the criminal process – such as the police, the Crown Prosecution Service (CPS) and the criminal courts. By looking at the stages, agencies and decision-making processes within the English Criminal Justice System, you will learn to understand how the various agencies work (or don't work) together. The criminal process of England and Wales is essentially *adversarial* in nature. You will find the terms 'adversarial' and 'inquisitorial' in your textbooks (the latter defines the Continental European Criminal Justice System). Their meanings cannot simply or precisely be defined, but these terminologies reflect particular historical developments rather than the practices of modern legal systems. In broad terms, adversarial justice (England) refers to the common law system of conducting proceedings in which the parties have the primary responsibility for defining the issues in dispute and for investigating and advancing the dispute (not the judge – as in France or Germany). An adversarial Criminal Justice System offers a 'party prosecution' of a dispute under the common law system; this means that parties (i.e. the Crown Prosecutor and Defence Lawyer) present the facts to the court. The term 'inquisitorial' refers to civil code systems (e.g. Spain or Greece) in which the 'inquisitorial' judge has such primary responsibility.

Core areas: **Structure and organisation of the Criminal**

System: an overview

The Criminal Justice agencies

Recent changes in Criminal Justice policies

Fear of crime

Race and hate crime.

Learning outcomes

By the end of this section you should be able to:

- Recognise and demonstrate an awareness of the workings of the Criminal Justice System and its major criminal justice agencies
- Understand and analyse official crime statistics
- Be aware of penal policies
- Appreciate the public fear of crime phenomenon
- Comprehend the power of the mass media and how crime is represented by the media
- Demonstrate an understanding of what is meant by race and hate crime and be able to give examples in learned debate.

Running themes

- Human rights
- Fear of crime
- Victims of crime (Victimology)
- Punishment
- Inequality
- Globalisation
- Gender
- Punishment
- Crime and the media.

Structure and organisation of the Criminal Justice System: an overview

To understand the criminal process you need to know which Criminal Justice agencies have the power to arrest, bring a prosecution and punish. After a person has been arrested (the suspect), the prosecution (the Crown Prosecution Service – CPS) proceeds by way of summons where the suspect is given a date for first appearance in a Magistrates' Court. If the CPS proceeds with an arrest, a police officer has the power to grant bail to the suspect offender without going to the police station ('street bail', Part 2 *Criminal Justice Act 2003* (CJA 2003)). Most commonly, the suspect will be interviewed at the police station. The suspect is then charged (or not) and may be remanded in police custody.

Under the CJA 2003, the CPS determines the charge (not the police). Under the *Police and Criminal Evidence Act 1984* (PACE) there is a legal duty to bring the defendant before a court as soon as possible; usually the next day. The police may bail the defendant to court or keep him in custody (s 38 PACE). There is a fundamental right to bail (*Bail Act 1976*). The CPS then reviews each charge (case file) and applies the 'public interest' test in favour (or not) of proceeding with the prosecution.

The choice of charge/s determines the mode of trial. If the charge is serious (rape, murder) the case will go to the Crown Court on indictment. Most charges are summary and tried only in the Magistrates' Court. Triable-either-way offences (an intermediate category of offences) may be tried at a Magistrates' or Crown Court. This is the defendant's choice. The 'Plea Before Venue' procedure involves the defendant being asked whether he pleads guilty or not. If he pleads guilty, Magistrates take charge of the case and may proceed to sentence, if they believe their sentencing powers are adequate enough. If the case is triable-either-way and serious, Magistrates may commit the case to Crown Court. When the defendant has pleaded not guilty, there is a 'Plea and Directions Hearing' which defines issues to be addressed at trial by defence counsel and prosecution (e.g. is the case long and complex? How many witnesses need to be called? Any interpreters? etc – ss 39–43 *Criminal Procedures and Investigations Act 1996*).

A defendant convicted by Magistrates or found guilty by the jury in a Crown Court trial will then be punished by form of a sentence. This can involve a fine (e.g. motoring offences), community punishment administered by the Probation Service (e.g. shoplifting) or prison administered by the Prison Service (e.g. serious fraud; manslaughter; robbery). A life sentence is given for murder or 'grievous bodily harm' with Intent (s 18 *Offences Against the Person Act 1861* (OAPA)).

The Criminal Justice Agencies

- The Police
- The Crown Prosecution Service (CPS)
- Magistrates' Courts
- The Crown Court
- Prison & Probation Services (National Offender Management Service–NOMS).

You will see that there is a large body of statutory legislation. Below, you will find a general overview of the most important Acts of Parliament:

Criminal Justice Acts

- *Offences Against the Person Act 1861 (OAPA)*
- *Children and Young Persons Act 1933*
- *Murder (Abolition of Death Penalty) Act 1965*
- *Theft Act 1968*
- *Criminal Damage Act 1971*
- *Misuse of Drugs Act 1971*
- *Bail Act 1976*
- *Magistrates' Court Act 1980 (MCA)*
- *Mental Health Act 1983*
- *Police and Criminal Evidence Act 1984 (PACE)*
- *Drug Trafficking Offences Act 1986*
- *Road Traffic Offenders Act 1988*
- *Road Traffic Act 1991*
- *CJA 1991*
- *CJA 1993*
- *Criminal Justice and Public Order Act 1994*
- *Bail (Amendment) Act 1994*
- *Criminal Procedures and Investigations Act 1996*
- *Offensive Weapons Act 1996*
- *Protection from Harassment Act 1997*
- *Crime and Disorder Act 1998*
- *Human Rights Act 1998 (HRA)*
- *Youth Justice and Criminal Evidence Act 1999*
- *Terrorism Act 2000*
- *Proceeds of Crime Act 2002*
- *Anti-Social Behaviour Act 2003*
- *Sexual Offences Act 2003*
- *CJA 2003*

Recent changes in Criminal Justice policies

Over the past decade or so, Britain has seen the most rapid changes in Criminal Justice policies and a wealth of new legislation. One of the key targets set by the New Labour Government since 1997 has been to increase the confidence of the public in the Criminal Justice System and to alleviate the **fear of crime** element, only enhanced by the **media**. The *Crime and Disorder Act 1998* (CDA) has taken full account of **victims** and **inequality** (inequality and the economy; marginalisation and crime relationships). **Globalisation** aspects of crime have involved criminological research into the following: the (mis)representation of crime; crime and social development; crime and social dysfunction; crime as choice; and crime control. Victims of crime can now be compensated by court 'Reparation' or 'Compensation' orders under the 1998 Act. Not only do the police have the power to **punish** offenders, but also local authorities, in the form of Anti-Social Behaviour Orders (ASBOs).

You will need to be aware of recent changes in criminal justice legislation. These are as follows:

- Criminal Justice and Public Order Act 1994 – *created new public order offences; no right to bail for defendants charged with rape or homicide; new offence of 'male rape'.*
- Protection from Harassment Act 1997 – *putting people in fear of violence.*
- Crime and Disorder Act 1998 – *introduced a range of criminal and civil orders, plus nine new offences related to hate and racially motivated crime.*
- Criminal Justice Act 2003 – *introduced a vast body of legislation (not all has come into force yet) e.g. 'bad character' (previous convictions or 'antecedents') can now be mentioned in court before/during a trial; Magistrates' sentencing powers have increased; one generic Community Sentence; abolition of double jeopardy (a person can now be tried again for the same criminal offence).*

Among the more radical of the Government's 'law and order' initiatives has been the introduction of Restorative Justice (RJ). RJ is about victims, where offenders have to 'make good' their crime towards the victim, rather than being solely prosecuted by the state. RJ attempts to strike a balance between the concerns of victims and their communities and the need to find an effective way of reintegrating offenders into society. Section 2.3 deals with Restorative Justice in more detail.

Criminal Justice statistics

There are a number of primary source crime statistics: official police statistics (reported crime) and crime-victim surveys. The latter is an important primary source of information, because victims do not always report crime for various reasons. Without these crime-victim surveys, governments would have no information on these unreported crimes. One of these is the British Crime Survey (BCS) conducted by the Home Office. The BCS is about levels of crime and public attitudes to crime. The results play an important role in informing government policy. The BCS measures the amount of crime in England and Wales by asking approximately 9000 people anonymously about crimes they have experienced in the last two years. This establishes the dark figure of crime, i.e. crimes that are not reported to the police; this makes the BCS an important alternative to police records. The BCS moved to an annual cycle from 2001/02, with 40,000 interviews of people aged 16 or over now taking place per year. For more details on the BCS, see page 25.

Then there is the International Crime Victim Survey (ICVS) the most far-reaching programme of standardised sample surveys to look a house-holders' experience with crime, policing, crime prevention and feelings of unsafety in a large number of countries. The ICVS provides information on crime and victimisation through a standard questionnaire, the results of which are internationally comparable.

The ICVS to date

There have been five rounds of the ICVS. The first was developed by a working group set up in 1987, and was done in 14 countries by 1989, led by the Ministry of Justice in the Netherlands in co-operation with the UK Home Office and the University of Lausanne in Switzerland. The second ICVS sweep took place in 1992, using face-to-face interviews as well as the Computer Assisted Telephone Interviewing technique (CATI); there were by now 33 participating countries. The third round was in 1996/97 totalling 48 countries (12 industrialised nations, all but one of the countries in Central and Eastern Europe plus 15 developing countries). The fourth sweep was done in 2000 in 47 countries, with the United Nations Interregional Crime and Justice Research Institute (UNICRI) being responsible for surveying and co-ordinating the developing countries, and the Ministries of Justice and Foreign Affairs of The Netherlands, the UK Home Office and UNDP Baku (Azerbaijan) responsible for the remaining nations. Specific research concentrated on 'Crimes against Businesses' in five Eastern-Central European countries and a global study on the 'Illegal Drug Markets' in 20 cities worldwide with missions undertaken to Bogota, Istanbul, Cairo, Johannesburg; Tokyo, Bangkok, New Delhi, Lima, Rio de Janeiro, Peshawar and La Paz. The fifth round of ICVS survey was done in 2004/05, including the 15 old Member States of the EU, carried out in part by Gallup/Europe. Additionally, 20 other countries were surveyed, including Argentina, Mexico, USA, Canada, Australia, New Zealand, Japan, China, Switzerland, Norway, Slovenia, South Africa, Estonia and Poland.

To date, over 140 surveys have been done in over 70 different countries. The BCS and the ICVS help to identify those most at risk of different types of crime, and this helps in the planning of crime prevention programmes. These surveys look at people's attitudes to crime, such as how much they **fear crime** and what measures they take to avoid it. They look at people's attitudes to the Criminal Justice System, including the police and the courts.

The British Crime Survey (BCS)

This survey is carried out in England and Wales. It started in 1982, with the BCS 2000 being the eighth survey. The BCS 2000 was carried out by the Social Survey Division of the Home Office and the National Centre for Social Research. One person (aged 16 or over) is selected, at random, for interview at each selected address. There are two self-completion sections at the end of the questionnaire and the respondent is encouraged to do these on a laptop. The last BCS was in 2003–04 (Home Office Statistical Bulletin 07/05).

BCS topic areas include:

- Experiences of crime – property and personal
- Attitudes to the Criminal Justice System, including the police and the courts
- Worries, fears about crime
- Security, including neighbourhood watch, home and vehicle security measures
- Violence at work
- Perceptions of equality and prejudice
- Volunteering and community activity
- Experience of household fires
- Illegal drug use
- Sexual victimisation.

Some results from the BCS

- Crime has fallen steadily since 1998 ('down' by about 12% since 2000)
- 33% drop in crime (2000–04)
- 27% of adults are victims of crime (39% in 1995)
- Young men (aged 14–24) are five times more likely to become victims of violent crime
- Risk of over 65-year-olds being victims of crime is very small (0.5%)
- 13 million crimes committed – four times the rate reported to the police (2000).

Reported ('recorded') crime

The official police recorded crime reports and statistics provide a good measure of trends in well-reported crimes. They are an important indicator of police workload and performance (e.g. clear-up rates) and can be used for local crime pattern analysis. This statistical series covers all 'notifiable' offences recorded by the police and notified to the Home Office, known as 'recorded crime'. This does not mean all criminal offences, but almost all the *summary* offences are included. The crime recording process is governed by three key stages:

Reporting a crime: someone reports to the police that a crime has been committed or the police observe or discover a crime or crime-related incident.

Recording a crime: the police decide to record the report of a crime and now need to determine how many crimes to record and what their offence types are. The Home Office issues rules to police forces on the counting and classification of crime. These 'Counting Rules for Reported Crime' are fairly straightforward, as most crimes are counted as 'one crime per victim' and the offence committed is obvious (e.g. domestic burglary). However, it also covers special situations where more than one offence has taken place, maybe on several occasions over a period of time, or there is more than one offender or victim.

Detecting a crime: once a crime is recorded and investigated, and evidence is collected to link the crime to a suspect, it can be detected according to criteria contained in Home Office counting rules ('Detection Guidance'). In many cases, someone is charged or cautioned or the court has taken the offence into consideration (TIC). The Detections Guidance covers these detection methods as well as certain others where the police take no further action. The last available reports were in 2004–05 and can be found on the Home Office 'Research, Development and Statistics Development' (RDS) website and A – Z index: www.homeoffice.gov.uk

---

Common pitfalls:

- Do not base your knowledge on what you read in the popular press
- If you are quoting statistics, use 'official' ones, such as recorded crime figures (by the police), or victim surveys (Home Office; British Crime Survey (BCS); self-reported victim studies)
- Note that crime statistics do not tell the whole story and often conflict with each other
- Be aware that all official crime surveys encounter problems concerning the estimation of levels of crime.

Official crime statistics, such as recorded crime by the police and victimisation surveys (British Crime Survey – Home Office) include only violent behaviour and offences that closely fit national legal definitions of crime (e.g. assault or grievous bodily harm contra ss 47 or 20 Offences Against the Person Act 1861 *OAPA).*

Fear of crime

Fear of crime is a very prevalent issue today and is made worse by the media. Despite the fact that official Home Office figures have shown a significant drop in the overall level of crime, fear of crime amongst the general population is still on the increase. This is largely attributed to the influence of the media. The fear of crime phenomenon has gained momentum over the past 20 years.

When this issue first came about, researchers became interested in it as a source of discovering the 'dark figure' of crime, i.e. unreported crime. Victim surveys, like the British Crime Survey (BCS), conducted by the British Home Office every couple of years, establishes the dark figure of crime by interviewing approximately 9000 victims of various crime categories anonymously; the results are then theorised and related to experiences of victimisation. Some of the results and assumptions are disputed. Researchers have recognised that numerous factors and variables play a role in the fear of crime.

Fear of crime can be defined as an anticipation of victimisation, rather than fear of an actual victimisation. This type of fear relates to how vulnerable a person feels. Gender has been found to be the strongest predictor of fear. Women have a much greater fear of crime than men, but, according to the BCS, are victimised less than men. Women's fears centre on their vulnerability and on sexual aggression (e.g. rape). Women are not born with this inherent fear but they are socialised into thinking that they are vulnerable to an attack, for example, if they go out alone at night. Parents, peers and media emphasise and reinforce this fear, and women are expected to succumb to it.

Age is also a powerful predictor of fear and varies from crime to crime. The elderly are the most afraid of, say, being mugged or burgled. When it comes to crimes like sexual assault and stranger attacks (stalking), it has been found that younger people tend to be more fearful. The vulnerability of the elderly stems from the physical and social limitations that elderly people have, which renders them unable to defend themselves or to seek support and help.

Certain crimes generate more fear than others. Being a victim of a robbery, for example, generates a high level of fear because it contains elements that cause a greater amount of fear to be instilled in its victims. Robbery usually involves a stranger, weapons, physical assaults and the loss of a fair amount of money. Burglary, because of its invasion of privacy and substantial amount of loss, generates a high level of fear.

Crime and the media

The media tends to sensationalise certain crimes, e.g. crimes against the elderly; crimes against children (paedophilia) and child pornography on the Internet.

According to the International Crime Victimisation Survey (ICVS), victims generally express the most fear of walking alone in their neighbourhood after dark. After this comes being a victim of sexual assault, followed by robbery, burglary, assault, vandalism, motor vehicle theft and personal theft. Fear of crime also varies according to where one lives. People who live in cities tend to hold higher levels of fear because cities and other urban areas tend to have higher crime rates than rural areas.

Fear of crime statistics

- *Today's crime levels are lower than ten years ago (a drop of about 4% each year)*
- *Young males are most likely to be victims of crime (17% of 14–16 year olds are victims of assault compared with 4% of over 65 year olds)*
- *Many crimes go unreported: the dark figure of crime (42% of rapes)*
- *Public opinion of fear of crime shapes governmental and penal policy.*

In terms of ethnicity and cultural background, the ICVS has found that fear levels vary according to ethnic background. While white respondents tend to show the least amount of fear, the question of who has the most fear has not been unanimously agreed upon. The BCS 1994 found that in relation to crimes of harassment, burglary, rape and mugging, the 'Asian' group expressed the most fear. The 'Black' group showed the next highest fear level in relation to these crimes, while the 'White' group showed the least amount of fear.

Governments have tried various fear-reducing measures in the form of a wealth of Criminal Justice legislation, and law-enforcement agencies have been increasingly called to action. There are a number of neighbourhood watch areas and community policing schemes today. Private security has increased and is now a big, profitable industry where wealthy housing estates are constantly patrolled in order to make residents feel more 'safe' and ultimately reduce people's fear. Foot patrol, using a large number of Police Community Support Officers (PCSOs), has been a method of policing since 2003, aimed to reduce crime and fear of crime. PCSOs interact with the community and make themselves seen – getting to know the people of the area. Research has found that the presence of these PCSOs has left people less fearful.

Fear of crime facts

- *Crimes people fear most: burglary (32%); assault (28%); rape (18%); mugging (13%); terrorism (11%) –* Observer *opinion poll 2003*
- *Although crime figures have been falling since 1999, public fear of crime is increasing*
- *Fear of crime is bigger than crime itself*
- *Women are significantly more afraid of crime than men (64% vs 47% – BCS 2003)*
- *Certain crimes are enhanced by the media (against the elderly and children)*
- *The dark figure of certain crimes is considerable (true levels of crime) (i.e. 50% of all crime goes unreported; Home Office British Crime Surveys)*
- *Actual extent and nature of crime is highly under-estimated*
- *Domestic violence is common (crimes within families)*
- *Elderly abuse represents a large dark figure (in the domestic and care home setting)*
- *Old people are more fearful than the young*
- *Crimes against the elderly by strangers are quite rare.*

When writing about 'crime and the media' you may wish to make the following points:

- *The media impact influences public opinion about crime*
- *Popular press reports often distort and sensationalise true images of crime*
- *Victimisation of certain individuals (e.g. children) increases public fear of crime.*

Race and hate crime

Race and hate crimes pose a serious social problem that scholars and policy-makers have argued is, in many ways, more threatening to civil society than other types of crimes. These crimes tend to be very brutal, especially in the case of bias against persons due to their sexual orientation, race, or gender. Homophobia, for instance, is a hate crime and can be defined as prejudice or discrimination against lesbians, gay men and bisexual people. A homophobic incident is any incident that appears to be related to an individual's actual or perceived sexuality.

In race and hate crimes perpetrators select their victims based on bias not against that individual but against a whole group with which that individual is associated. These types of crimes tend to be committed by multiple perpetrators, a feature contributing to their severity and brutality. Due to their very nature, race and hate crimes bring about particularly high levels of psychological stress, fear and anxiety, where victims are often powerless to protect themselves since it is difficult or undesirable to disguise their inherent identities.

Race (or racist) and hate crime can take the following forms:

- Racially abusive behaviour
- Causing damage to property outside gay venues
- Circulating or displaying racist or homophobic material
- Offensive graffiti
- Physical violence
- Assaults where the perpetrator's actions or words display a homophobic motive
- Verbal abuse
- Incidents in which heterosexual people, mistaken for homosexual or bisexual people, are subjected to homophobic abuse, harassment or attacks
- Domestic violence in a heterosexual setting (e.g. where a husband beats his wife after having discovered she is a lesbian).

Some race crimes concentrate on specific geographical areas and can lead to wider neighbourhood division and social fragmentation. Once such example was the killing of Stephen Lawrence in 1993. The 17-year-old black teenager was stabbed to death in Elthams, South-East London – as he was waiting at a bus stop with his friend one Thursday night. The Macpherson Inquiry (1997) established that the police reacted far too late to the 999 telephone calls for help.

After all suspects were cleared of Stephen Lawrence's murder at the Old Bailey trial in February 1997, the *Daily Mail* cleared its front page and identified – by name and photographs – five white youths whom it accused of murdering the black teenager. The paper noted that this criminal case had come to an end without justice being done.

Another such example was the murder of Damilola Taylor. The brutal killing of the black ten-year-old on a South London council estate in Peckham in November 2000, shocked the British public. The boy had been left bleeding to death in an alleyway of the housing estate. Although all four suspects in the murder investigation, all under the age of 17, had previously been known to the police as street bullies and running junior forms of protection rackets in South London, the London Metropolitan Police could not convict any of the four teenage suspects, for allegedly mobbing the boy for his silver jacket and fatally stabbing him to death with a cut-glass bottle, due to poor and inconclusive evidence. The two main defendants in the trial, suspect brothers known as Boy A and Boy B of 'Mediterranean origin', were cleared of all charges at the Old Bailey Crown Court trial on 25 April 2002. The 12-week trial of Damilola's alleged killers and the police investigation cost £2.8 million.

" Is the fear of crime justified? "

For this answer you need to refer to official crime statistics (see above) and use websites e.g. Home Office (British Crime Surveys), and police statistics to back your answer. You need to mention that the fear of crime amongst the public is higher than crime itself, and give reasons for this (e.g. the media 'hype' of certain crimes which don't necessarily reflect true crime statistics).

" What is the aim of the Criminal Justice System? "

In your answer you could mention: to deter offenders; to deliver retribution; to rehabilitate offenders.

" What is meant by 'racially motivated' or 'hate crime'? "

You need to define the terms firstly in law and then give some examples such as the Damilola Taylor or Stephen Lawrence killings.

" What is meant by 'victimless' crime? "

Describe firstly what is meant by victims and describe the research in this area (Victimology). Then explain crimes such as social security or insurance fraud.

Taking it **FURTHER**

If you want to look up and read about Criminal Justice statutory legislation, consult *Blackstone's Statutes on Criminal Law* (latest 14th edn, edited by P.R. Glazebrook, 2004).

The following are worth detailed reading:

1. Human Rights Act 1998
2. Crime and Disorder Act 1998
3. Criminal Justice Act 2003

Textbook guide

ASHWORTH, A. AND REDMAYNE, M. (2005) *The Criminal Process.* 3rd ed. Oxford: OUP.

BOWLING, B. AND PHILLIPS, C. (2002) *Racism, Crime and Justice.* London: Longman.

CARLEN, P. (ed.) (2002) *Women and Punishment: the struggle for justice.* Cullompton: Willan.

DAVIES, M., CROALL, H. AND TYRER, J. (2005) *An Introduction to the Criminal Justice System of England and Wales.* 3rd ed. London: Pearson/Longman.

ELLIOTT, C. AND QUINN, C. (2005) *English Legal System.* 5th ed. London: Longman/Pearson.

WALKLATE, S. (2004) *Gender, Crime and Criminal Justice.* 2nd ed. Cullompton: Willan.

2.2	
understanding crime and criminal law	

This section is divided into two areas: Criminology and criminal law. Both are very important to your study. The first part introduces you to sociological and criminological theories that deal with distinctions between crime and deviance. You will be introduced to theories that consider *why* a person may become deviant and a criminal youth, and *how* the environment (i.e. family or school) has a major influence on the causes of crime and criminal behaviour. Do not be put off by some of the jargon and 'criminological' speak! This section explains specific criminological terms and theories in, hopefully, a user-friendly way. If you would like to learn more about criminological theory, please refer to the Sage Course Companion on Criminology (Treadwell, 2006).

The second part of this section provides you with the basic building blocks to what makes up a criminal offence in English criminal law: the *actus reus* and the *mens rea*. We will focus on the meaning of *intention* and you will learn to reflect on the difficult notion of *recklessness*.

Core areas: **Making distinctions between crime and deviance**
The changing nature of criminal offences
Criminal law: building blocks of a criminal offence.

Learning outcomes

By the end of this section you should be able to:

- Make distinctions between crime and deviance

- Understand the multi-disciplinary approach of Criminal Justice and Criminology

- Ask questions about crime and the purpose of criminal law

- Demonstrate a basic knowledge and appreciation of what constitutes a criminal offence

- Identify key issues surrounding the *mens rea* and *actus reus* elements to a crime.

Running themes

- Inequality
- Gender
- Criminalisation
- Punishment
- Human rights
- Victims of crime (Victimology)
- Fear of crime.

Making distinctions between crime and deviance

What is crime? A crime is an activity that is classified within the criminal laws of a country. English criminal law is partly common law – as in 'murder' and partly enshrined in statute. Criminal legislation on 'homicide' still rests with common law tradition ('judge-made' law) whereby legal precedents have been set by case law. Offences such as burglary, issuing false cheques, subscribing to a child pornography website, selling Class

A drugs, or having sexual intercourse with children are all statutory offences now. Graffiti, for instance, falls within the statutory criminal offence of 'criminal damage'.

Criminology deals with causes of criminal behaviour and teaches us to understand certain kinds of behaviour (e.g. why children become deviant and turn to crime). 'Deviance' is a classical theme in Criminology, where the causes of crime are explained. For example, Criminologists now perceive strong links between youthful offending and the home (*familial*) environment. You need to learn to distinguish between what is 'criminal' and what Criminologists call 'deviant behaviour' or deviance.

Passing an exam well in this area of crime, deviance and social control will mean that you are familiar with certain criminological and sociological terms. The following will assist you when you are asked to give a critical analysis *by way of a discursive essay or exam question ('critically analyse' or 'evaluate'):*

- **Norms***: social sets of specified behaviour patterns, e.g. religious norms give rise to heretics; legal norms to criminals; health norms to the sick; cultural norms to the eccentric etc. Norms emerge in most social situations*
- **Deviance***: a pattern of* norm violation. For example, there can be class deviance, *where the normative expectations of class behaviour are violated; or situational deviance, where the norms emerging between a group of friends are transgressed*
- **Stigma** *(pl. stigmata): deviance can be highlighted as a* stigma construct, a label *bestowed upon certain classes of behaviour at certain times, which then become devalued, discredited, and often excluded. This characteristic can also be seen as very wide-ranging: people may be regarded as possessing a deviant stigma, simply because they belch or talk too much. A more extreme example is that of* terrorists; *they may become political martyrs in the eyes of those who share their particular values (freedom fighters) whilst in the eyes of others and generally the criminal law, they are murderers. The study of deviance is concerned primarily with the construction, application, and impact of stigma labels*
- **Norm violation or stigma construct***: deviance is a shifting, ambiguous, and volatile concept. Precisely who or what is deviant depends upon a firm understanding of the norms and the* labelling process *in particular social contexts.*

When you are writing a criminological essay you may need to refer to causes of crime, deviance and social control. You need to do the following:

- *Refer to behaviour that is morally ('normatively') wrong*
- *Mention deviance and delinquency which can (but not necessarily do) lead to criminal behaviour*
- *Write about deviant 'behaviour patterns' such as: the delinquent; the homosexual; the mentally ill etc*

- Explain what is meant by 'dysfunctional family background' and how this may lead to criminal ('yob') culture and future criminal behaviour
- Refer to **inequality** factors, such as: coming from a broken home; being brought up by a single (or lone) parent – and how these factors can influence 'criminogenic' behaviour patterns
- Mention how **gender** issues may influence the decision-making process in the Criminal Justice System.

There are several competing criminological theories that focus on styles of criminal families. Glueck and Glueck (1950) compared 500 well-behaved schoolboys with 500 institutionalised delinquents; they discovered that 66% of the delinquents had a criminal father or brother, compared with 32% in the control group. Bowlby (1944; 1979) concluded that maternal deprivation through rejection was linked to childhood anti-social behaviour and later delinquency. Other theorists concluded that deviance and delinquent behaviour are learnt through observing and 'modelling' (imitating) others. Hirschi (1969), in his 'control theory', found that children from larger families were harder to discipline and likely to receive less parental attention than small families. Farrington et al. (1996) reasoned in their 'strain theory' Cambridge studies that delinquents were likely to come from families with four or more children. Other variables included low family income, demographic and socio-economic status which appeared to influence and indicate anti-social behaviour in their empirical studies.

You will do well if you learn and familiarise yourself with some of the most common sociological, psychological and biological theories in order to explain deviance and sources of criminal behaviour, i.e. why some individuals turn to crime and some do not.

That said, you need to treat such criminological research results with great caution. Some American and Swedish (twin and adoption) studies revealed that criminological (biological) behaviour runs in the family, there is an equal number of studies that persuade us otherwise.

Common pitfalls:

- Take great care not to generalise
- Not every youngster with a dysfunctional family background turns criminal

- Not all family break-ups or 'lone parenting' are causes of crime
- Economic deprivation and **inequality** (i.e. working class or poor background) do not always lead to crime.
- Most poor or working-class people are law-abiding citizens
- Most young criminals commit minor crimes (but the 'dark figure' is substantial, i.e. they don't get caught)
- Beliefs about human nature are often 'smuggled' into theories and treated as 'obvious'; these need to be looked at carefully and critically
- Don't stereotype people in an attempt to create explanations (e.g. it is often claimed that economic deprivation is a cause of crime; yet most poor people are not criminals)
- Understanding why crimes occur does not necessarily help us treat offenders or run crime prevention programmes
- Always back up your argument by citing learned literature (not the popular press).

Key thinkers

- **Karl Marx** (1818–83) born in Trier, Germany, he worked as a journalist in Paris (1843), Brussels (1845) and London (1848). His major work is *Das Kapital* (Capital), where he argued that the property-less class was being exploited which would lead to the class struggle over the distribution of economic resources. See also: Marx and Engels (1848) *The Communist Manifesto*. London/Harmondsworth: Penguin. A classic for all those who wish to understand the basics of Communism.
- **Robert K(ing) Merton** (1910–) born in Philadelphia USA. He wrote about the *dysfunctional* aspects of *bureaucracy* and was one of the first social scientists to reveal the inefficiencies as 'red tape' related to bureaucracies. He also theorised about *crime and punishment*. Merton proposed the theory of *anomie*, suggesting that when someone cannot attain the goals of society using acceptable means, this person will likely attain the goals in a socially unacceptable way (normlessness), resulting in criminality (see Merton's 'Social Structure and Anomie', in *Social Theory and Social Structure*, 1968), Merton's work is also related to *strain theory*. *Strain* is the frustration felt by an individual in society and the sense of injustice that results from experiencing socially structured incapacities as low capabilities; this meant the frustration between material wealth and well-being in comparison with poverty. He focused on the 'American Dream' society and the stress on material goods common in the 1930s and '40s society, such as the low incomes of most workers (European 'old money' versus American 'new money').

The changing nature of criminal offences

Over the past decade, Britain has seen a plethora of new penal policies in form of Criminal Justice and process legislation. Significant changes in respect of the **punishment** of persistent young offenders were made under the *Crime and Disorder Act 1998* (CDA). Penal policies and resulting changes in criminal law are usually consequences of wider social policies and changes in political and social life; these in turn will influence law enforcement priorities (such as policing). Legal definitions of crime and criminal offences change with time and place. Below are some of the most common criminal offences that are worth quoting in an assessed essay:

Burglary

According to the British Crime Survey (BCS) 2004, the domestic burglary rate has been steadily falling since 1999.

Vehicle crime

This offence usually involves 'joy-riding' or 'Taking a vehicle Without the Owner's Consent' (known as 'TWOCing'). There has been a steady downward trend since 1997.

Alcohol-related crime

This usually involves assaults (domestic violence and pub fights).

Violent crimes

Recorded violent crime (by the police) includes: robbery; sexual offences; and 'violence against the person' offences (ss 47; 20; 18 OAPA 1861). Violent crime has increased since 2003 and now dominates the British crime scene.

Domestic violence

Most victims of domestic violence are women who suffer on many levels: health, housing and education. Domestic violence is chronically under-reported.

Robbery and street crime

Robbery (commonly called 'mugging') and snatch-theft are both types of street crime. Though the Home Office reports that overall levels of crime have been falling steadily (by about 3–5% since 2000), there has been a worrying increase in the level of certain violent offences since 2004, such as street robbery, thefts of mobile phones and serious assaults.

Football disorder (hooliganism)

This is a type of subcultural criminality that has been associated with English football for over 100 years. Football hooliganism may not be as prevalent as it once was, but it remains a serious menace, particularly in international matches.

Drugs and crime

There are strong links between drug use and crime. Around three-quarters of crack and heroin users claim they commit crime to feed their habit. The problems of drug misuse are complex and require integrated solutions and co-ordinated delivery of services involving education, intelligence and enforcement, social and economic policy, and health. There has been an increase in police activity aimed at drug dealing over recent years.

Sexual offences

Until recently, sexual offences were very much under-reported. Since the Government's high profile TV and radio advertising campaign in 2004, sexual offences are now reported more frequently to the police. Law enforcement agencies are now dealing better with **victims** of sexual crimes.

Internet and cybercrime

Internet crime is a phrase used to describe a range of different crime types, from child pornography to fraud. The statistical picture regarding this type of sophisticated crime is limited. Terms used in this area of criminal offending are: cybercrime, e-crime and hi-tech crime.

Identity fraud

This refers to the misappropriation of the identity of another person, without their knowledge or consent, and falls in the offence category of 'white collar crime'. ID fraud is a **global** operation. The stolen information (such as credit card theft) is used to obtain financial services, goods and other forms of identification. ID fraud usually involves the use of stolen or forged identity documents (e.g. passports). The information is obtained by burglars from people's dustbins, such as utility bills, national insurance numbers, driving licences or credit card bills. CIFAS, the UK's Fraud Prevention Service, reported that there were some 20,000 reported cases of ID fraud in 1999, and that this increased to 101,000 in 2003. The worst ID fraud is undertaken by 'data brokers' who hack into banks, computers and sell the information they have trawled.

Common pitfalls: When writing an essay on understanding crime and crime rates remember the following:

- Be careful not to generalise: the idea of 'crime' covers a large variety of human behaviours
- Not all crimes can be explained in the same way
- Legal definitions of crime are not usually useful starting-points for trying to understand or explain human behaviour
- It is often more helpful to start with sociological descriptions of 'deviant' acts and 'deviant' social statuses
- Changes in the number of people processed through the Criminal Justice System can be influenced by a number of factors unrelated to the level of crime or the numbers of crimes cleared up
- Statistical 'flows' through the Criminal Justice System vary with police, prosecution and court statistics
- Don't forget to mention police clear-up rate and conviction rates
- Detection rates vary widely according to types of offences; they are generally highest for violent crimes.

Criminal law: building blocks of a criminal offence

This section introduces the reader to the general principles of criminal liability and criminal law. It is generally believed that those who act involuntarily do not deserve punishment, nor would their **punishment** serve any useful purpose. An individual who lacks control over his (criminal) actions is generally not regarded as being responsible for the consequences of those actions and incurs no criminal liability. English criminal law describes these actions as 'automatism'.

Unless otherwise stated, all criminal cases start with 'R v ...' (i.e. Regina or Rex in older cases pre-dating Queen Elizabeth) – that is The Crown against an accused individual before the criminal courts. Most precedents are made in the Criminal Court of Appeal (CA) or the House of Lords (HL). For the purpose of finding a legal case you may wish to look these up either in a law library, a criminal law textbook, or on the Internet using the database LEXIS/NEXIS (Butterworths).

The actus reus *element and causation of a criminal offence*

'Actus non facit reum nisi mens sit rea' – An act does not make a man guilty of a crime unless his mind is also guilty.

In establishing liability for a criminal offence, the prosecution must prove that the defendant possessed both the *actus reus* and the *mens rea* to the criminal offence.

Actus reus – the defendant (D) has performed a harmful conduct or behaviour towards a victim (V) as defined in or by the offence.

Mens rea – the state of mind of the defendant at the time of the *actus reus*. It looks at intention.

A person is innocent until proven guilty: the burden of proof lies firmly with the prosecution to prove the prisoner's guilt. (*Woolmington v DPP* [1935])

The burden of proof

- *The burden of proof lies with the prosecution*
- *The Golden Thread theory: 'Throughout the web of the English Criminal Law one golden thread is always to be seen, that it is the duty of the prosecution to prove the prisoner's guilt ... No matter what the charge or where the trial, the principle that the prosecution must prove the guilt of the prisoner is part of the common law of England and no attempt to whittle it down can be entertained.' (extract taken from Viscount Sankey's speech in* Woolmington v DPP *[1935] HL)*
- *The evidential burden: the prosecution must adduce enough evidence of an allegation against the defendant to enable the courts to allow the issue to be heard and examined*
- *The defendant never has to prove anything (unless statute says so!).*

- *Coincidence of* actus reus *and* mens rea*: prosecution must prove that* mens rea *existed at the same time as the* actus reus *of the crime*
- *The defendant may bring evidence to show that he had no* mens rea *for the crime he is charged with*
- *The defendant may admit that he had* mens rea*, but raise a general defence (e.g. duress; self-defence; automatism)*
- *Some crimes require knowledge of certain circumstances as part of the* mens rea *(e.g. receiving stolen goods requires knowledge that they were stolen)*
- Strict liability *crimes require no* mens rea.

There are regrettably no specific legal definitions for crimes of basic and specific intent. Therefore, we have to rely on common law, as Lord Simon stated in *DPP v Morgan* [1976] – the classic case which set the precedent for the 'mistaken belief' in rape cases:

A *basic intent* crime is one whose definition specifies *mens rea* that does not go beyond the *actus reus*, that is the act and its consequences.

Basic intent crimes include:

- *Manslaughter*
- *Criminal Damage*
- *Non-fatal offences against person (e.g. assault, s. 20 OAPA)*
- *Rape.*

Crimes of *specific intent* are often referred to as 'ulterior', 'hidden' or 'concealed' crimes, where the *mens rea* goes beyond contemplation of the *actus reus*. Specific intent crimes require proof of some *purposive element*.

Specific intent crimes include:

- *Murder*
- *Grievous bodily harm with intent (s. 18 OAPA)*
- *Theft (*Thefts Acts 1968 *and* 1978*).*

> **Common pitfalls:** When answering a criminal law or problem-type question:
>
> - Take care when you are asked about the *burden of proof*
> - The general rule is: *the prosecution* must prove that the defendant committed the offence (to prove your point, you need to cite *Woolmington v DPP* [1935] AC 462) – and here it is worth citing the principle of the 'golden thread theory' as established by Viscount Sankey)
> - The *standard of proof* rests with the prosecution: that a crime must be proven *beyond reasonable doubt* (i.e. beyond a shadow of a doubt) that the defendant is guilty of the alleged offence
> - The only time the defendant has to put forward evidence is when he is using a *defence* to murder (e.g. provocation or self-defence)
> - *Reverse burden of proof* is on the defendant when it is written in statute (e.g. in terrorism offences such as those under the *Terrorism Act 2000*).

The kind of questions likely to arise in your criminal justice exams include:

- Questions about social processes leading particular individuals towards or away from crime
- Questions about the socio-patterning of offending (why does one social group have a higher proportion of offenders than another social group?)
- Questions about the relationships between politics, law enforcement, social norms, and offending.

The following questions deal with the difference between 'crime' and 'deviance', and address the criminological issues in this section:

❝Why and how do individuals become involved in criminal activities?❞

❝How and why do individuals cease to become involved in criminal activities?❞

Here are some suggestions how to answer this type of question, and the following concepts will help you construct a good argument. The kind of factors often considered important in constructing explanations in the field of causes of crime and deviance are as follows:

- The socialisation of young people and their social interaction among adults in particular environments is important for their personal development
- Economic and social deprivation can (but not necessarily does) lead to crime

- Proportionately more young offenders than young non-offenders come from broken homes
- During late adolescence and vocational training, family background takes second place and new 'social authorities' take over (job; university; unemployment).

"To what extent is the criminal law a reflection of a society's morality?"

You need to reflect on social changes and how society views crimes today compared with, say, after the First and Second World Wars (e.g. bicycle theft). You need to mention some new criminal offences which have been created by statute (e.g. terrorism legislation; drug trafficking; human trafficking; prostitution etc). You have to distinguish between what is morally wrong and against the (criminal) law, and how this might differ from country to country. Refer to interrelationships between law, social norms, definitions of deviance, law enforcement, power, and offending and deviance. Ask why some behaviours are defined as offences in one jurisdiction but not another, or at one period in history but not others.

Taking it *FURTHER*

1. Look up the following words in a (criminological) dictionary and write down their meaning:
   dysfunctional; social behaviour and practices; cultural beliefs; incarceration; discipline; surveillance; total institutions; anomie.
2. Look up the following cases; they all raise the *actus reus* of manslaughter. In each case you need to examine the notion of *intention* and then ask yourself: was there a duty to act?, and if so did the defendant fail to act when s/he was under a duty to do so? (known as an act of *omission*).

   - *Gibbins and Proctor* [1918] 13 Cr App R 134; 82 JP 287 – Examines the notion of 'parental duty' towards their children.
   - *Stone and Dobinson* [1977] 1 QB 35; 2 All ER 341 – Duty of care towards relatives.
   - *Adomako (John Asare)* [1995] 1 AC 171 [HL] – A doctor's (anaesthetist) duty of care to the victim (a patient during an eye operation); test for gross negligence manslaughter.
   - *P&O European Ferries [Dover] Ltd.* [1990] 93 Cr App R 72 – Duty of care of a company towards its passengers; corporate manslaughter.

Textbook guide

ASHWORTH, A. (2003) *Principles of Criminal Law.* 4th ed. Oxford: Oxford University Press (OUP).

HALE, C., HAYWARD, K., WAHIDIN, A. AND WINCUP, E. (eds) (2005) *Criminology.* Oxford: Oxford University Press (OUP).

HEATON, R. (2004) *Criminal Law.* Oxford: OUP.

HERRING, J. (2005) *Criminal Law: text, cases, and materials.* Oxford: OUP.

MARTIN, J. AND TURNER, C. (2005) *Unlocking Criminal Law.* Abingdon, Oxon: Hodder & Stoughton.

MCLAUGHLIN, E. AND MUNCIE, J. (eds) (2005) *The Sage Dictionary of Criminology.* London: Sage.

WILLIAMS, K.S. (2004) *Textbook on Criminology.* 5th ed. Oxford: OUP.

2.3

punishment and sentencing framework

This section gives you a general idea of the main punishment theories. Once you have learnt these theories, you need to apply them to today's sentencing procedures, as Magistrates and judges do every day. You will learn how these punishment theories (e.g. 'Deterrence' or 'Rehabilitation') translate into Criminal Justice policy and thereafter into Criminal Justice statutes, and how the criminal process reflects such theories.

Though some of the theories presented here might initially be quite wordy, they are worth learning. Therefore, pay particular attention to the **Tips!** features in this section; they will help you memorise some of the new and possibly unfamiliar terms in this context of study. There are now vast ranges of sentencing options available to the courts, particularly in the form of the new and generic 'Community Sentence' which came into force in April 2005 under the *Criminal Justice Act 2003*.

Core areas: **Punishment theories and sentencing paradigms**
Retribution and 'just deserts'
Deterrence
Rehabilitation
Incapacitation
Restorative justice
Sentencing practice in the courts

Learning outcomes

By the end of this section you should be able to:

- Distinguish between legal and moral approaches to punishment
- Define and understand the range of punishment theories
- Establish the link between punishment theories and practical sentencing decision-making in the criminal courts
- Define major punishment theories in Criminal Justice legislation.

Running themes

- Punishment
- Human rights
- Criminalisation
- Victims of crime (Victimology)
- Inequality
- Globalisation

Punishment theories and sentencing paradigms

There are a number of different theories of punishment. They all have different aims and purposes and are the basis for sentencing provisions in the criminal courts today. Justices have to bear these punishment concepts firmly in mind when they sentence a convicted criminal. They ought to be aware of society's need for a **humane** system of Criminal Justice in the *Human Rights Act 1998* (e.g. 'right to a fair trial' or 'freedom from inhumane and degrading treatment').

Many philosophers (e.g. Immanuel Kant) have defined the meaning of 'punishment':

i)   It must involve unpleasantness

ii) It must be for an offence

iii) It must be for an offender

iv) It must be the work of a criminal justice agency

v)   It must be imposed by an authority.

Theorists like John Rawls have distinguished between 'formal justice' (the law) and 'material justice' (morality and politics); they have argued that these two concepts are overlapping. Criminologists like David Garland (1990) have also described 'social justice' as dealing with the 'goodies' and the 'baddies' in our society and how they ought to be punished. A notable distinction is usually drawn between social (*distributive*) justice, and *retributive* justice. Retributive justice (see *Retribution* on p. 47) believes that the guilty should be punished simply because they have done wrong.

Key thinkers

- **Immanuel Kant** (1724–1804) – Born in Königsberg, East Prussia (Germany), Kant never travelled more than 50km outside his home. Kant is one of the most influential philosophers. His most influential work is *Kritik der reinen Vernunft* (1781) (*The Critique of Pure Reason)* where Kant's work addresses the question 'What can we know?' – the advancement of knowledge, including reflections on crime and punishment, which he treated as 'freedom of the mind' (to commit crimes). Kant argued that 'criminal man' has to take the consequences of his actions and expect punishment for his wrong-doing as an indispensable practical function.
- **John Rawls** (1921–2002) – Born in Baltimore, Maryland, USA, Rawls developed the concept of justice and the 'difference principle', which asserts the notion of **inequality** and the (unfair) distribution of scarce goods in society

(power, money, access to healthcare, etc). *A Theory of Justice* (1971) is very theoretical text, but essentially the book is about Rawls' theory of 'justice as fairness', which rests on three principles: (1) the principle of equal liberty – each person is to have an equal right to the most extensive system of equal basic liberties compatible with a similar system of liberty for all; (2) the principle of equality of fair opportunity in that positions are to be open to all, under conditions in which persons of similar abilities have equal access to office; (3) the difference principle – this requires social and economic institutions to be arranged so as to benefit maximally the worst-off.

- **Jeremy Bentham** (1748–1832) – Born in Houndsditch, London, Bentham was known as a leading radical in Anglo-American philosophy of law. He is the founder of *utilitarianism* which evaluates human actions based on the philosophy of 'happiness for all'. The utilitarian school believed that all punishment is evil, insofar as it adversely affects human happiness. Bentham's utilitarian theory of punishment is often cited in the context of *Deterrence* (see Bentham's *Introduction to the Principles of Morals and Legislation*, 1789). He is famous for the 'model prison' the *Panopticon* (see section 2.9 'Prisons'), where all prisoners would be observable by (unseen) guards at all times, a project which he had hoped would interest the Czarina Catherine the Great. By the late 1790s, Bentham had considerable influence on continental penology and advised on vast prison building programmes. He was made an honorary citizen of the new French Republic in 1792.

Retribution and 'just deserts'

Retribution or *Retributivism* is one theory of punishment. It involves a fair allocation of Criminal Justice – known as the 'just deserts' theory. The concept of retribution implies that a criminal merits his just punishment, since he has done something morally, socially or criminally wrong. An aspect of retribution implies that the punishment should be related to the harm done by the crime, rather than to the moral guilt of the criminal: the punishment must fit the crime, i.e. the sentence for the convicted criminal must be commensurate with his offence/s.

The *Criminal Justice Act (CJA) 1991* has been regarded as one of the most positive legislative frameworks, reflecting the retributive punishment theory in the form of its sentencing structure that is available to justices. Its underlying aim was to ensure that sentences are proportionate to the seriousness of the offence of which the offender stands convicted (punishment must fit the crime). Some of these positive forms of sentencing have now been overturned by the CJA 2003.

How then is retribution translated into sentencing practice by the courts today? Justices (Magistrates or Crown Court Judges) have to ask themselves: Is the punishment we are about to give in the form of a sentence, appropriate and a just response to the crime committed? Does the punishment fit the crime? (e.g. in the form of a community sentence). Will the convicted criminal get his just deserts? Sentencers then look at past offending (*antecedents*) and the defendant's past offending behaviour patterns.

Deterrence

Although simple in conception, *deterrence* theory can be extremely complicated in sentence practice. It often reflects a penal policy where the government attempts to control the behaviour of other actors by the use of threats. The 'deterrer' (the state) then tries to convince the 'deterree' (the criminal) that the costs of undertaking the actions that the deterrer wishes to prevent will be substantially higher than any gain that the deterree might anticipate making from the action.

Deterrence means:

- *Punishment aimed at deterring the criminal from repeat offending*
- *Preventing future crimes; or*
- *Reducing the likelihood of a similar offence being committed in future*
- *Fear of punishment (anticipation penalty)*
- *'Unpleasant' sentences (e.g. prison)*
- *Encouraging the public to be law-abiding citizens*
- *Offender should 'stop and think' about consequences of their actions ('If I rob this bank, will I be caught and punished?')*
- *Justified sentencing to prevent greater harm to society*
- *Deterring others from committing similar acts*
- *Addressing the criminal's future offending behaviour in its sentencing*
- *Harsher (longer or more punitive) sentences on repeat offenders* (recidivists).

The deterrence-type sentence becomes weaker and more ineffective, the more an individual is punished. Research has established the more deeply a person becomes involved in criminal activity, the harder it will be to reform them. This is particularly the case with habitual, life-long criminals, persistent (young) offenders, generally known as recidivists. Deterrence in Criminal Justice policies has meant that longer and harsher sentences were introduced, as well as tariffs and mandatory sentences for certain offences (CJA 1993 for murder and rape). The 'short, sharp, shock-treatment' was reflected in CJAs 1982 and 1988, and managed to have some success rate with first-time criminals. However, this specific approach had little meaningful effect on reconviction rates.

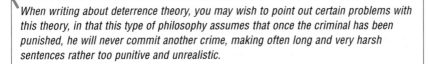

When writing about deterrence theory, you may wish to point out certain problems with this theory, in that this type of philosophy assumes that once the criminal has been punished, he will never commit another crime, making often long and very harsh sentences rather too punitive and unrealistic.

Rehabilitation

The sentencing formula of *rehabilitation* focuses on the rehabilitation of the offender (e.g. *Rehabilitation of Offenders Act 1974*). Here sentencers make every effort to change the offender's future behaviour, so that he can lead a 'useful and crime-free life' after being in custody or having served a community sentence. It is believed by rehabilitative theorists that the offender needs professional support to achieve this (e.g. the Probation Service). Most rehabilitative sentencing today involves alternatives to custody, in the form of the generic 'Community Sentence'.

The term *decarceration* is often used in this context. This involves the process of removing people from institutions (such as prisons or mental hospitals) and sentencing the offender to a programme of community care.

Rehabilitation means

- *Non-custodial punishment*
- *Community Sentence or community care (Probation)*
- *Drug or alcohol treatment orders*
- *Sex Offender Treatment programmes*
- *Anger management programmes*
- *Home Detention Curfew (electronic tagging).*

Incapacitation

Incapacitative theories identify particular groups of offenders (e.g. burglars) who do serious harm to society. Incapacitation theorists believe that certain criminals need to be removed from society for a long time. Incapacitation was used by Mayor Rudolph Giuliani in his 'zero tolerance' policy in New York during the mid-1990s; thereafter adopted by the first Labour Home Secretary, Jack Straw in 1997, as a basis for the *Crime and Disorder Act 1998*. The result was longer sentences for serious offences (including repeat burglary; street robbery; and sexual offences).

You may wish to point to the difficulty with this theory. Incapacitation means sentencing criminals with future objectives in mind – e.g. the longer you keep a burglar in custody, the fewer burglaries will be committed during that time, and insurance claims will go down. Given this theory, some criminals will therefore never be released from prisons (for example, violent paedophiles or serial killers will be kept in prison under a natural life sentence).

Restorative justice

The *restorative justice* (RJ) theory concentrates on **victims of crime**. RJ demonstrates the need for the offender to 'make good' to the victim in the form of reparation or compensation (rather than to society). This model is closest to the rehabilitative theory. One form of RJ is victim-offender mediation, thought to change the offender's future way of thinking. Under the *Crime and Disorder Act 1998*, the Probation Service offers face-to-face contact with victims of crime as well as with their offenders (if so requested). The *Powers of Criminal Courts [Sentencing] Act 2000* and the *Criminal Justice Act 2003* substantially increased the sentencing powers of Magistrates in this area. RJ has been successfully and widely applied in youth justice and sentencing in the Youth Courts (*Youth Justice and Criminal Evidence Act 1999*).

Restorative justice (RJ) involves:

- *Victim-offender mediation*
- *Reparation and compensation to victims of crime*
- *Offenders taking responsibility for their actions*
- *Offenders making amends to their victims and communities*
- *Victims being consulted and informed about offender's release from prison*
- *Addressing future behaviour of the offender.*

How do courts decide on a sentence?

- They must consider an appropriate level of sentence where the punishment must fit the crime
- The level of punishment (sentence) must be based on the seriousness of the offence (low, medium or high risk offence?)

- Is a fine appropriate? If so, size of fine?
- Is a Community Sentence appropriate? If so, how many hours of unpaid work?
- Will only custody suffice? If so, how long for a prison sentence?
- Is a discharge sentence appropriate? If so, absolute or conditional?

The *European Convention on Human Rights and Fundamental Freedoms* (The Convention – ECHR 1950) as incorporated into UK law by the *Human Rights Act 1998* on 2 October 2000, forbids the use of 'inhumane or degrading' treatment (i.e. punishment) and Art. 7 ECHR sets out the prohibition on the use of arbitrary punishment.

❝ Compare and contrast 'retribution' and 'restorative justice' with relation to sentencing legislation. ❞

You need to address theories of punishment here and specifically define the meaning of the two given terms. Firstly, **retribution**, defined as 'an eye for an eye' – where society imposes punishment by pain and humiliation upon the criminal, regardless of his crime. Retribution is one theory of punishment and the content of criminal law in western societies is based on this theory. Some of the most obvious and important of these conditions include respect for basic **human rights**, such as the rights not to be intentionally killed or physically harmed by anyone.

With **restorative justice** (RJ), crime is treated as an inescapable part of society, including the **global** aspects of crime (e.g. economic deprivation; cost of city living; expected effect of social chaos etc).

Retribution tells us little about what a particular defendant's sentence ought to be, or even how to define a range of acceptable punishments for a given crime. Courts then make sentencing choices about fairness and proportionality whereby the punishment should fit the crime within the **global** pattern of possible sentences. You should focus on (and give examples of) sentences for specific offenders (e.g. burglary or assault) and the necessary sentencing involvement by justices and given reasons for their decisions.

❝ 'The death penalty should be introduced for people who kill police officers' – Former Chief Constable of West Yorkshire (1993–98), Keith Hellawell told BBC News on the evening of 27 December 2003, after Police Officer Ian Broadhurst was shot in a quiet street in Leeds. Discuss, with reference to punishment theories surrounding imprisonment. ❞

The **death penalty** is a controversial topic and has been for a number of years. **Capital punishment** was abolished in the UK in 1965, but still exists in a number of countries (e.g. it was reinstated in the United States during the 1970s in a number of states such as California and Texas). Whenever the word 'death penalty' comes up, you will find that extremists from both sides of the spectrum begin to express their opinions; especially on the Internet. One side says deterrence, the other side says there is the potential of executing an innocent person. You need to address both sides of the argument in a learned and scholarly fashion.

 Taking it *FURTHER*

Look up David Garland's (1990) *Punishment and Modern Society: a study in social theory.* David Garland is an eminent academic in punishment theories; this is an approachable reader and gives you an insight into modern ways of public attitudes to punishment and theoretical thought.

Textbook guide

CAVADINO, M. AND DIGNAN, J. (2001) *The Penal System. 2nd ed. London: Sage.*

EASTON, S. AND PIPER, C. (2005) *Sentencing and Punishment: the quest for justice. Oxford: OUP.*

GARLAND, D. (1990) *Punishment and Modern Society: a study in social theory. Oxford: Clarendon.*

HUNGERFORD-WELCH, P. (2004) *Criminal Litigation and Sentencing. 6th ed. London: Cavendish.*

MARSH, I. (2004) *Criminal Justice: an introduction to philosophies, theories and practice. London: Routledge.*

MCCONVILLE, S. (ed.) (2003) *The Use of Punishment. Cullumpton: Willan.*

VON HIRSCH, A. AND ASHWORTH, A. (2005) *Proportionate Sentencing: Exploring the Principles. Oxford: OUP.*

2.4	
police	

This section focuses on police and the changing role of the police force over the past years. One of the main areas of study is the *Police and Criminal Evidence Act 1984* (PACE) which provides important measures for police officers' powers of arrest, dealing with stop and search, interview and arrest procedures at the police station. This will include changes under the PACE Review 2002.

Community policing will then be highlighted in line with recent government crime prevention strategies, whereby large amounts of resources have been allocated to the recruitment of Police Community Support Officers (PCSOs) in order to tackle local and street crime as well as anti-social behaviour.

Your attention will be drawn to recorded crime statistics, crime and police efficiency measured in clear-up rates. It is important to remember that crime levels are influenced by social, economic and cultural factors. We will also be looking at policing styles ('cop culture') and the growth in private policing.

Core areas: **Policing: past and present**
Crime control and efficiency
Extent of police powers under PACE
Institutional racism
Community and reassurance policing
Private policing
The future of policing.

Learning outcomes

By the end of this section you should be able to:

* Understand the need for social order by policing
* Be aware of and define the multi-faceted approach of police activity today

- Be familiar with the extent of police powers and the boundaries of police work set by PACE in line with human rights legislation
- Identify what is meant by 'zero tolerance' policing
- Define what is meant by 'community policing' and give examples
- Appreciate what is meant by 'race', 'ethnicity' and policing
- Illustrate issues relating to private policing.

Running themes

- Fear of crime
- Human rights
- Race
- Globalisation
- Crime and the media
- Victims of crime
- Inequality

Policing: past and present

In 1829 Robert Peel introduced London's 'New Police' force. The 'thief takers' (like the 'Bow Street Runners') then controlled local disturbances and 'ungovernable' areas rather informally. A form of mixed economy policing developed with main forms of policing concentrating on the poor and socially deprived (**inequality**). Most prosecutions concentrated on property crime (burglary, sheep-taking, horse theft, etc). Arguably, nothing has changed today.

Today, the police remains the major agency of law enforcement in every country whereby governments pass and seek to enforce laws. Whilst the most common feature of English policing has been the community 'bobby' – this has changed as well. Reiner (2000) examined policing styles and distributed these along dimensions from 'soft' (community policing) to 'hard' or 'babylon' policing (teams carrying riot equipment). The latest introduction to community policing has been the Police Community Support Officer (PCSO) who may look like a police officer on the beat, but has no true powers under PACE – in some high crime areas, this is already known by young children.

The tasks of today's police force are varied and far-reaching. The balance between 'soft' and 'hard' policing has had to be readdressed, and the bobby has been largely replaced by PCSOs on the streets in order to alleviate the **fear of crime** and make the general population feel more 'safe' by increased 'police' presence.

Key thinkers

- **Robert Reiner** (1946–) – His research concentrates on the emergence of the police force and changing styles of policing. He first identified the police officer as society's 'peacekeeper', who sees his role as assisting the public. Reiner describes how police officers react to their job in a variety of ways, leaving sometimes the cynical and disillusioned 'uniform carrier' who is just waiting for his pension.

Crime control and efficiency

The importance of police efficiency and effectiveness measures increased dramatically from the late 1970s onwards, for a variety of reasons. EU countries have experienced a long-term increase in the rate of crime, in spite of the fact that crime rates began to fall from the late 1990s onwards. But, since 2002, according to the British Crime Survey, certain crimes have rapidly increased, such as street robbery and assaults. Meanwhile, we can observe a general drop in police clear-up rates (i.e. solving reported crimes). Police efficiency is measured in 'key performance targets' and below is a list which gives you some of these indicators:

What constitutes modern day effective policing?

- Quick responses to crime
- Maintaining public order by patrolling public areas
- Reassuring the public and making society feel safe ('Reassurance Policing')
- Crime prevention
- Dealing with public disturbances (demonstrations; football matches; strikes etc)
- Tackling anti-social behaviour ('zero tolerance' policing)
- Intelligence gathering
- Dealing with security issues (i.e. acts of terrorism).

Police clear-up rates

- *Suspects caught and charged*
- *Clear-up rates low and falling*
- *Fewer than 25% of all crimes are cleared up (in some forces fewer than 10%).*

Police efficiency is measured in crime reduction in a particular area. Falling crime rates can be measured by the amount of property crime, for instance. Generally, property crime has fallen over the past decade, some of the reasons are:

- Improved car alarms and immobilisers on new cars
- Improved household security (burglar alarms).

There has also been improved city centre surveillance by means of Close Circuit Television (CCTV) – and it can be said that criminals have actually moved away from household and car-crimes, and turned to new types of criminal offences such as white-collar crime (e.g. credit card fraud), Internet (cyber) crimes; stalking; sexual abuse and harassment. Criminologists will also have us believe that low unemployment rates reduce property crime.

Common pitfalls: When you are asked to write about reported (recorded police) crime rates, you need to be careful and point out to the examiner that 'official' crime rates can be confusing. You have to tell your reader that what is important is that levels of crime can only be truly determined by taking reported crime rates in conjunction with levels of unreported crime. This can be achieved by using other methods, such as victim surveys (British Crime Survey, Home Office). You need to stress that any research into the effectiveness of policing has to take other aspects into account: factors that might have influenced the crime rate at the time; whether deterrence was the most likely explanation. Bear in mind other processes, such as positive and pro-social developments (e.g. the opening of new leisure or youth facilities) or changes in public attitudes.

Extent of police powers under PACE

Prior to the *Police and Criminal Evidence Act 1984* (PACE), arrest and 'stop and search' matters were dealt with by a variety of statutes and common law. PACE sought to modernise and rationalise police law in the way police constables (PCs) conducted themselves in public. The 1984 Act sets out a PC's functions, powers of stop and search, and arrest, and gives discretion on the street by its various relevant sections.

PACE and its codes of practice (see below) are key elements of the framework of legislation, providing the police with the powers they need to combat crime. PACE has been seen as the most comprehensive piece of legislation governing police and citizens' rights and duties in modern times.

PACE Codes

- **Code A**: deals with the exercise by police officers of statutory powers to search a person or a vehicle without first making an arrest. It also deals with the need for a police officer to make a record of a stop or encounter
- **Code B**: deals with police powers to search premises and to seize and retain property found on premises and persons
- **Code C**: sets out the requirements for the detention, treatment and questioning of people in police custody by police officers
- **Code D**: concerns the main methods used by the police to identify people in connection with the investigation of offences and the keeping of accurate and reliable criminal records
- **Code E**: deals with the tape recording of interviews with suspects in the police station
- **Code F**: deals with the visual recording (with sound) of interviews with suspects.

PACE Codes were revised by the PACE Review 2002 in line with **human rights** legislation (*Human Rights Act 1998*). In doing so, PACE strikes the right balance between the powers of the police and the rights and freedoms of the individual.

PACE Review 2002

- *Extension of powers to stop and search* (s 1) – Now includes articles made, adapted or intended for use in criminal damage
- *Warrants to enter and search* (s 2) – Authorised people accompanying a PC are allowed the same powers of execution and seizure

- *'Street Bail'* – Bail elsewhere than at a police station (s 4) – Enables PCs to remain on patrol for longer periods; suspect need not be taken to police station
- *Use of telephones for reviews of police detention* (s 6) – Enables reviews of detention without charge to be conducted by telephone rather than in person
- *Limits on periods of detention without charge* (s 7) – Extends maximum time of detention for arrestable offence from 24 to 36 hours
- Magistrates' Court can issue warrant for further detention up to 96 hours (*Prevention of Terrorism Acts 1976* and *2002* and s 7 PACE Code 2002)
- *Property of detained persons* (s 8) – removes absolute requirement to make detailed records of a detained person's property
- New police powers introduced under Part I *Criminal Justice Act 2003.*

Aims and objectives of the Police and Criminal Evidence Act 1984 *(PACE):*

- *Gives PCs general powers to 'stop and search' a suspect (s 1(2) PACE)*
- *PC must have 'reasonable grounds' for stop and search (not just a hunch)*
- *Search warrants: search and seizure (s 8)*
- *Special procedure material (s 14)*
- *Arrestable offences (s 24): where sentence is fixed by law (e.g. murder) or for imprisonable offences (persons aged 21 or over – five or more years prison)*
- *Non-arrestable offences (s 25)*
- *Duty to give reason (s 28)*
- *Suspect's right to inform someone (s 56)*
- *Right to inform legal representative (s 58).*

Institutional racism

The popular concept that the police is 'institutionally racist' resulted from the inquiry into the killing of the black A-Level student, 17-year-old Stephen Lawrence in 1993. The inquiry's findings were published in the *Macpherson Report* (1999). Some of the findings were, that after the teenager was left for dead in Eltham, East London, the police did not attend after repeated phone calls from Stephen's friend. Eventually, criminal prosecutions against the initial five suspects failed. Not only did the *Macpherson Report* note the failings of the Metropolitan Police (the Met) by not following up immediately on Stephen's murder, but the inquiry also recognised that 'institutional racism' prevailed in the police force.

Chronology of the Stephen Lawrence killing

- 17-year-old black A-Level student Stephen Lawrence is murdered on 22 April 1993 at a bus stop in Eltham, East London
- Accused: a gang of white youths
- Police do not react fast enough to emergency calls made by Stephen's friend Duwayne Brooks who witnessed the murder
- Initially five suspects arrested (Neil and Jamie Acourt, Luke Knights, Gary Dobson and David Norris)
- Three suspects charged with Stephen's murder; tried and later acquitted (Acourt, Dobson and Knight)
- Two separate murder investigations and inquiry into the Metropolitan Police, prompted by Home Secretary Jack Straw and led by Sir William Macpherson
- *Macpherson Report* (1999) refers to 'institutional racism' in the police
- May 2004 CPS announces that there will be no further prosecutions in the Stephen Lawrence case (no clear, new (DNA) forensic evidence).

The fallout from the Macpherson inquiry forced the Met (and other police forces) to change the way they deal with race issues, such as racially motivated and hate crimes. The Report recommended strong pro-active strategies for the future of the police force to tackle racial violence and all 'hate crimes'.

Recommendations from the Macpherson Report (1999)

Records must be kept of *all* stops and searches, including:

- Reasons for stops and search
- Outcome of stop and search
- Self-defined ethnic identity (ethnicity)
- Copy of record must be given to person stopped
- Records must be regularly monitored, analysed and reviewed.

Following the *Macpherson Report* in 1999, the Home Office issued major penal policies by ensuring that the Criminal Justice System would be fairer for black and ethnic minority communities and that every police officer involved in them would give priority to **equal** and **humane** treatment of all suspects. The report had highlighted a police culture that had tolerated a workplace ethos of sexism and homophobic racism, as well as harbouring discriminatory working practices.

Have things changed in terms of more tolerant policing? Home Office figures published in July 2004 (BCS 2004) revealed that individuals from ethnic communities continue to be stopped and searched more regularly than white people. The most striking results were in stops and searches of Asian individuals post 9/11. The research showed that Asians being stopped and searched had risen by a staggering 302%. Reasons for this were attributed to Muslim terrorist activities on and post 9/11.

Police stops and searches

- Black people are six times more likely to be stopped and searched by police than white people (up by 38%)
- There are twice as many stop and searches of Asian people than white (s 44 PACE)
- Total stops and searches for Asians up by 302% (from 744 to 2989)
- Racist incidents fell by 11% (2002–03)
- Numbers of arrests: three times higher for black people than others
- 12% more racist incidents resulted in prosecution
- Black and minority ethnic groups highly under-represented in police force
- Although there was a disproportionate number of ethnic minority deaths in custody between 1 April 1998 and 31 March 2003, the disproportionality could not be directly related to racist attitudes or behaviour.

Source: British Crime Survey 2004, Home Office

The fact is that ethnic communities remain under-represented in the police force and that ethnic minorities are also more likely to be **victims of crime**. The BCS 2004 revealed one positive result: more people from ethnic minority and black communities than white, believe that the Criminal Justice System is now more effective in bringing people to justice and reducing crime in the fight against **globalised** and organised crime.

When writing a discursive essay about levels of crime, you need to cite your sources accurately. Here is an example:

The 2001 Census showed that nationally 2.8% of the resident population were Black, 4.7% Asian and 1.2% of 'Other' minority ethnic groups. The new Census figures used in 2003 (S95 Statistics) made direct comparisons with figures from the previous year. However, they were regarded us 'unreliable' since they did not compare like with like (Source: Home Office RDS Reference: 220/2004 – Date: 2 July 2004).

Community and reassurance policing

Today, greater partnership participation is expected from all sections of the community in the fight against crime. With the *Crime and Disorder Act 1998*, local authorities are co-operating more closely with other Criminal Justice agencies, particularly the police (but also social services, health services, schools; youth services, and Youth Offending Teams (YOTS) etc). But recent Home Office research evidence has shown that criminal **victimisation** is still higher per capita in deprived areas than affluent areas, highlighting continued social **inequality**.

Community or 'reassurance' policing is regarded as 'enhanced' police work and part of a wider PR (public relations) act. The National Reassurance Policing Programme (NRPP) was introduced in 2003; this used citizen-focused community policing strategies to target visible crime and disorder, in order to make neighbourhoods more secure. Local people in 16 sites across eight police forces in England were used to identify local crime concerns, as well as signal crimes.

Signal crimes

- *Some crimes and disorders act as warning signals to people about their exposure to risk*
- *These 'signals' impact on the public's sense of security*
- *They cause people to change their beliefs and/or behaviours to adjust to the perceived risk*
- *Perspective covers large spectrum of crimes and disorders; and*
- *Gives an opportunity to target those problems that matter most to the community*
- *Police and local partners establish 'control signals' to neutralise signal crimes and signal disorders.*

New Home Office guidelines now include community engagement, with local people taking ownership of their neighbourhoods in partnership with the police and other agencies by tackling signal crimes and disorders. The result was that by 2005, communities were feeling safer in the pilot areas. Community policing in the form of Police Community Support Officers (PCSOs) was also introduced in 2003. PCSOs gained greater powers under PACE from April 2005 onwards, in order to carry out stops and searches (e.g. use handcuffs).

What are Police Community Support Officers (PCSOs) used for?

- *Crime prevention and detection*
- *Visible street patrols*
- *Good PR: enhance public image of policing*
- *Deal with the drunk and disorderly; parking matters; neighbourly disputes; lost property; guarding crime scenes etc*
- *'Good' police work (e.g. domestic violence).*

Private policing

The **fear of crime**, reflected in neighbourhood 'crime talk' is today heightened by media hype of certain crimes, where limited personal experience and rumours are generalised or even **globalised**. So, who benefits from crime? How much will people pay to prevent crime? With a shift towards punishment and increased penal legislation in EU countries, private security measures have drastically expanded after 9/11. We now appear to live in a global terrorist culture in addition to our 'normal' everyday (property) crime.

Media-hyped crime-talk has enhanced the **fear of crime** and in spite of increased neighbourhood and community policing, there remains a general mistrust in law enforcers. There has been a vast growth in the private security industry, such as private policing and surveillance. But such new and private (or privatised) crime control arrangements are costly. Residents of certain wealthy residential housing developments spend a great deal of additional funds on security fencing, and employing security guards to create 'gated communities'. Some estates employ vigilante-style patrols, while some not-so-rich estates have taken the law into their own hands, since their trust in local police forces has declined. Private security is now regarded as a privilege contained in the 'exclusive' British culture.

Private Security means:

- *Private policing*
- *Virtual reality surveillance (CCTV)*
- *Business watch*
- *Pub watch*
- *Neighbourhood watch.*

The future of policing

The nature of **global** and international policing has changed post the 9/11 terrorist attacks in New York and Washington – law enforcement has had to take on a more world-wide and multi-agency task force approach in order to combat international terrorism. The 9/11, Madrid 2004, and London transport bombings of 7 and attempted bombings on 21 July 2005 are blamed on the Islamic militant organisation Al-Qaeda, led by Saudi-born dissident Osama Bin Laden. Some experts say that since the Afghanistan war in 2001, Al-Qaeda has split into a loosely knit network of groups who have declared 'holy war' on Americans, Jews and their European allies. Others say Al-Qaeda has become an ideology for a certain type of virulent anti-western militancy.

Whilst the British police was one of the last vestiges not carrying guns, this has had to change. The days of Dixon of Dock Green and the traditional British bobby on the beat have gone. Inner city areas like Nottingham have introduced gun-carrying police officers with the intention of reassuring the public and sending a strong message to young criminals not to use guns. But the public **fear of crime** has increased nevertheless. Putting more armed officers on the streets is a very sensitive issue for Chief Constables, who are well aware of the public's unease.

There is no doubt that in recent years people in Britain have become more used to seeing police officers carrying guns. The weapons are a visible deterrent to terrorists at airports like Heathrow, inner city centres, or at major trials such as at the Old Bailey. Almost every police force now has armed response vehicles, ready to go to the scene of a robbery or siege. But still, the British force is a world away from the US or most European states (e.g. Holland or Germany), where the armed police officer is a fact of life, and most forces have paramilitary-style SWAT teams on call for major incidents.

When presenting a discursive essay about modern style policing, you can advance the following arguments:

- *Increasing the number of police officers does not necessarily reduce crime rates or increase detection rates*
- *Police forces cannot deal with the causes of crime but can only attempt to deal with the effect and suppress it*

- *Only a limited degree of crime suppression is possible using the kinds of police strategies in force at any given time, however well they may be resourced*
- *Large increases in the number of PCs on patrol in one particular area may reduce crime in that area, but usually crime 'displaces' itself to a nearby neighbourhood*
- *Neither vehicle nor PC foot (or bicycle) patrols are particularly effective methods for deterring or detecting offenders*
- *Fast response to crime does not increase the chances of detecting the offenders or make a difference to the clear-up rates*
- *Criminal investigation is not an effective way of solving crimes – if victims/witnesses cannot provide names or descriptions of offenders (e.g. car license plate), the likelihood of detection is very small*
- *Police–public relations have been poor, therefore, public confidence in police is low*
- *Police forces now put stress on 'alternative methods' i.e. using informers and encouraging suspects to 'assist police with their inquiries' (i.e. to admit further offences).*

Though a very different police force has emerged from its origins some 150 years ago, we are left with the relative ineffectiveness of the police in dealing with and preventing crime. After all, crime is caused by a variety of social conditions, not all of which can be tackled by the police alone. Since police forces mainly deal with the symptoms or results, not the causes, of such problems, it still takes greater community initiatives to assist the police in combating crime.

The future of policing

- *Range and type of police work is wide, varied and complex, including:*
- *Crime prevention and detection*
- *'Zero tolerance' and 'reassurance' styles of policing*
- *Maintenance of public order (crowd control, demonstrations etc)*
- *Community policing (Police Community Support Officers)*
- *Success depends on public co-operation and confidence*
- *'Joined up' justice (local council, youth offending teams, schools, social services, health services etc).*

Policing policies are increasingly driven by an international and **global** agenda dictated by national security, terrorism and internationally organised crime (drug trafficking, human trafficking, terrorism etc). In European

Union (EU) terms, the third (and initially weakest) pillar of the EU (justice and home affairs) was strengthened by the Nice (2000) and Rome (2004) Treaties. British police co-operation is linking up with international criminal intelligence agencies (Interpol and Europol). International legislation now facilitates easier extradition of criminals from one country to another ('European Arrest Warrant' – *Extradition Act 2003*).

“What are today's global issues of policing?”

You need to define the meaning of 'global'. Since criminals appear to ignore national boundaries, you need to state reasons why this is so, and what international law enforcement agencies are doing about chasing up organised crime and criminals (e.g. Europol, Interpol). What are the dangers of the opening of European borders?

“Is today's British police force racist? Discuss.”

Your starting point is the Stephen Lawrence–Macpherson Inquiry; you may also cite some other examples where the police have not acted immediately when a black person has been attacked or murdered. From the *Macpherson Report*, you need to identify key issues in policing today (e.g. stops and searches of more black or Asian people than white) and cite some Home Office statistics to back your argument. You may wish to examine police recruitment over the past five to six years, and how, particularly the Metropolitan Police Force/s have tackled the notion of institutional racism.

“What are the current powers under PACE for Police Officers and Police Community Support Officers (PCSOs)?”

You need to cite (summarise) the general statutory powers under the *Police and Criminal Evidence Act 1984* (PACE) – and you need to concentrate specifically on the powers of stop and search, arrest, warrants, and how long a suspect can be kept at a police station for questioning. It is worth noting the influence of the *Human Rights Act 1998* on PACE. Furthermore, you need to introduce the function and role of PCSOs and their (extended) powers under PACE. Finish your essay by a learned criticism and observations as to how PCSOs are perceived by the public/media.

Textbook guide

BOWLING, B. AND PHILLIPS, C. (2002) *Racism, Crime and Justice. London: Longman.*

LEISHMAN, F., LOVEDAY, B. AND SAVAGE, S. (eds) (2000) *Core Issues in Policing. London: Longman.*

NEWBURN, T. (2003) *A Handbook of Policing. Cullompton: Willan.*

REINER, R. (2000) *The Politics of the Police. 3rd ed. Oxford: OUP.*

ROWE, M. (2004) *Policing, Race and Racism. Cullompton: Willan.*

WILSON, D., ASHTON, J. AND SHARP, D. (2001) *What Everyone in Britain Should Know about the Police. London: Blackstone.*

2.5

prosecuting crime

In this section you will firstly be presented with a brief history of the Crown Prosecution Service (CPS) and how and why it was brought about in 1986. Secondly, you will learn all about the role of the Crown Prosecutor, his role in a criminal trial, and how a police suspect may be charged under the guidelines of the 'Code for Crown Prosecutors'. The CPS Code addresses the main issue of whether charging the criminal will be in the public interest or not and whether (police) evidence is sufficient to bring about a successful prosecution.

Core areas: **The emergence of the Crown Prosecution Service (CPS)**

Role and functions of the CPS

The Code for Crown Prosecutors

The evidential and public interest tests.

Learning outcomes

By the end of this section you should be able to:

- Identify and understand the role and function of the Crown Prosecution Service (CPS) in relation to the other Criminal Justice agencies
- Demonstrate some basic knowledge of the CPS Code of Practice; and
- Appreciate the importance of the evidential and public interest tests
- Identify the part played by the Crown Prosecutor in a criminal trial.

Running themes

- Human rights
- Inequality
- Victims of crime (Victimology)
- Gender.

The emergence of the Crown Prosecution Service (CPS)

By the beginning of the 1980s it became clear that some police forces (although not all) and certain police officers and detectives were corrupt. Certain forces had come under political pressure to make arrests, often resulting in wrongful convictions. The use of police informers was commonplace and pressure on certain under-cover officers frequently resulted in their illegal threats against informants or use of them to provide fabricated evidence. Corruption had emerged where officers were frustrated by legal processes ('noble cause' corruption, for example, where suspects are 'framed'), or where organised crime could 'buy off' the police.

One such case, involving the Surrey Police, was the *Guildford Four* (Paul Hill, Carole Richardson, Gerard Conlon and Patrick Armstrong), convicted of pub bombings on behalf of the IRA in Guildford and Woolwich. Police interrogation and investigative strategies were found to be gravely at fault (*May Report* 1993). Such situations became very difficult to unravel. For this reason the power to take criminal cases from first arrest to charge through the criminal courts was taken away from the police and the Crown Prosecution Service (CPS) was created in 1986 (*Prosecution of Offences Act 1985*) in order to avoid any further miscarriages of justice (Walker and Starmer, 1999).

From 1986 onwards, until the introduction of the *Criminal Justice Act 2003*, the CPS acted as an 'intermediary' authority between a suspect's first arrest by the police and the correct charging process with a criminal offence. From 1 April 2005 (CJA 2003), this decision-making process was simplified – the CPS now lays all charges and acts as an advisory capacity to the police. Practically, this means that a CPS representative is located in most police stations to speed up the charging process.

Role and functions of the CPS

The CPS is part of the Civil Service under the supervision of the Attorney General (AG). By September 2004, 35 of the 42 CPS areas were operating 'shadow charging'. This occurs where the Association of Chief Police Officers (ACPO) have agreed to accept the decision of the prosecutor; police agreement to charges are now not required. Statutory charging will be completed by 1 April 2007 (amendment to s 37 PACE by Sch. 2 CJA 2003). This means that the prosecutor (and no longer the police) decides that a suspect should be charged or cautioned. The police no longer have the power to charge (except for very minor cases). The prosecutor also recommends bail or a necessary remand in custody. It is here that the 'Threshold Test' will be applied in line with **human rights** legislation (Arts 5 and 6 ECHR) as well as s 37A(1)(a) PACE.

It is at the Magistrates' Court (MC) where *Mode of Trial* decisions are decided by the prosecution. In triable-either-way offences the defendant is asked whether he wants to have the case tried in the MC or wishes to pursue his case in the Crown Court. In serious charges, involving murder, sexual offences or grievous bodily harm, the prosecutor will always recommend a Crown Court trial on *indictment*, as soon as he is satisfied that the Code for Crown Prosecutor's guidelines require him to do so; in which case the Magistrates will commit the defendant to the Crown Court. Speed must never be the only reason for asking for a case to stay in the MC. Prosecutors must consider the effect of any likely delay if they send a case to the Crown Court and they should always take the **victim's** (and witnesses') interests into account.

The CPS

- **Responsibility for all prosecution decisions**
- **Each individual case is reviewed by prosecutor in Criminal Justice Unit (CJU)**
- **Police must provide evidence (information that affects decisions)**

- **Public interest test must be applied (Code for Crown Prosecutors)**
- **Proceedings can be stopped**
- **Prosecution can be restarted at any time (if new (DNA) evidence comes to light)**
- **Prosecution must consider children's interest (as defendants and victims/ witnesses).**

The Crown Prosecutor may not always continue with the most serious charge where there is a choice, meaning that he should not continue with more charges than are necessary. Furthermore, he should never go ahead with more charges than are necessary just to encourage a defendant to plead guilty to a less serious one. The Code tells him that he should not change the charge simply because of the decision made by the MC (or the defendant) about where the case will be heard in either-way offences. Defendants may want to plead guilty to some, but not all, of the charges, or they may want to plead guilty to a different, possibly less serious charge because they are admitting only part of the crime (this is called 'plea bargaining'). Prosecutors should only accept a defendant's plea if they think the court is able to pass a sentence that matches the seriousness of the offence; they should never accept a guilty plea just because it is convenient.

Plea bargaining involves:

- *Defendant may want to plead guilty to some, but not all, charges*
- *Defendant may want to plead guilty to a different/less serious charge*
- *Defendant may only admit part of the crime.*

The Code for Crown Prosecutors

The most recent changes of the Code and the full text of the revised *Code for Crown Prosecutors* (16 November 2004) can be found on the CPS website: www.cps.gov.uk. Section 10(1) of the *Prosecution of Offences Act 1985* provides that:

> The [Director of Public Prosecutions – DPP] shall issue a Code for Crown Prosecutor giving guidance on general principles to be applied by them.

The Code is under constant review in line with legislative and policy changes. It covers the following key areas:

- General Principles: a pro-active approach to case-building
- Review: the decision to prosecute
- The Threshold Test ('Evidential Test')
- Public Interest Factors ('Public Interest Test')
- Charges
- Mode of Trial
- Diversion from Prosecution
- Prosecutor's Role in Sentencing and Accepting Guilty Pleas
- Re-starting a Prosecution.

General Principles

- *CPS is the principal prosecuting authority (not the police)*
- *Independence in decision-making (including international and **global** dimensions of prosecuting)*
- *Pro-active case building: each case is unique and must be considered on its own merit*
- *The right person must be prosecuted for the right offence*
- *All relevant facts must be taken into account and given to the court*
- *Crown Prosecutors must be fair, independent and objective (i.e. must not let their personal views influence their decisions – defendant's ethnic or national origin; sex; religious beliefs; political views; sexual preference of offender, victim or witnesses)*
- *Prosecutors must not be affected by improper or undue pressure from any source.*

Review and the Evidential Test

- *Involves decision whether to prosecute or not; whether there is a 'realistic prospect of conviction'?*
- *If there is sufficient evidence, CPS will proceed*
- *Can the evidence be used?*
- *Is the evidence reliable?*
- *What is the defence's case?*
- *How is this likely to affect the prosecution's case (objective test)?*

Threshold Test

- *Balance all factors for and against prosecution (e.g. is there medical evidence?)*
- *Is there reasonable suspicion that the suspect committed the crime?*
- *Prosecution must always take place in serious charges (unless there are public interest factors against prosecution, e.g. matters of national security).*

Public Interest Tests

- *Factors in favour of prosecution (e.g. children or community offence, domestic violence)*
- *Some factors may increase the need to prosecute (e.g. offence against police officer or nurse)*
- *The more serious the offence, the more likely prosecution has to apply public interest test (e.g. acts of terrorism)*
- *All public interest factors must be put to the (Magistrates') court for consideration.*

Public interest factors *in favour* of a prosecution include:

✓ When a conviction is likely to result in a significant sentence

✓ When a weapon was used

✓ An offence against a child

✓ Domestic violence in front of children

✓ When violence was threatened during the offence

✓ An offence committed against a person serving the public (e.g. police or prison officer, nurse)

✓ A defendant in position of authority or trust (e.g. teacher, carer)

✓ Evidence showing that defendant is a ringleader or organiser of offence; or

✓ An offence which was premeditated; or

✓ An offence which was carried out by a group or gang

✓ When the victim was vulnerable (e.g. children); or

✓ The victim has been put in considerable fear; or

✓ The victim suffered personal attack, damage or disturbance

✓ An offence motivated by any form of *discrimination* against victim's ethnic or national origin; sex; religious beliefs; political views or sexual preference

✓ A marked difference between actual or mental ages of defendant and victim

✓ Evidence of corruption

✓ When the defendant's previous convictions/cautions are relevant to present offence

✓ When the defendant committed offence whilst under an order of court (e.g. bail)

✓ A repeat offence (i.e. history of recurring conduct)

✓ When an offence, though not serious, is widespread in area where committed.

Public interest factors *against* a prosecution include:

✓ When the court is likely to impose very small penalty

✓ When the defendant is already subject of a sentence (or in prison)

✓ When any further conviction is unlikely to result in an additional sentence

✓ An offence committed as result of genuine mistake or misunderstanding

✓ When loss or harm was minor and result of single incident (misjudgement)

✓ When there was a long delay between offence taking place and trial date (*unless*: offence was serious; delay caused partly by defendant; offence only recently came to light; complexity of offence meant long investigation)

✓ When a prosecution is likely to have a very bad effect on victim's physical or mental health

✓ When the defendant is elderly or suffering from significant mental/physical ill health (unless offence very serious or defendant will repeat offence)

✓ When the defendant has put right loss or harm caused (*Restorative justice*; victim compensation)

✓ When details made public could harm sources of information (e.g. national security).

Diversion from prosecution

- *Caution and Conditional Caution (Part 3 CJA 2003, ss 22–27)*
- *Alternatives to prosecution (where appropriate).*

Re-starting a prosecution

In rare cases the CPS may wish to restart a prosecution (Part 10 CJA 2003). Reasons include:

- Fresh look at original decision shows that it was *clearly wrong* and should not be allowed to stand
- New/fresh/significant evidence has become available (e.g. DNA)
- CPS must tell defendant that prosecution may start again.

In conclusion

Reasons for starting the CPS in 1986 were to create a new independent prosecuting body, with a move to the CPS for charging suspects instead of the police. The *Criminal Justice Act 2003* has enhanced the role of the prosecutor, in order to avoid 'cracked trials' which have cost the state approximately £41 million each year. Some see this penal policy move as stripping the police of its powers to charge suspects in favour of lawyers' approval. It was the Government's intention to bring about a more 'joined up' Criminal Justice System with the *Prosecution of Offences Act 1985*. It can be said that the relationship between the police and the CPS will never be the same as, say, between a defence lawyer and his client.

Bad character evidence

The *Criminal Justice Act 2003* allows the adduction of a defendant's bad character ('antecedents' or 'previous convictions') in court (ss 98 and 112). This was previously only possible in common law (and statutory rules) if the defendant had either pleaded guilty or he had been found guilty by Magistrates or by the Crown Court jury. The threshold of bad character adduction is now generally permitted *before* conviction if the defendant's bad character relates to the current charge of offence/s. In certain circumstances, this might even allow for a co-defendant's previous bad character to be adduced (ss 101–104 CJA 2003) (e.g. offences of dishonesty).

Common pitfalls:

- When answering questions on the CPS, avoid unnecessary waffle and stick to the CPS Code
- Answering this type of question involves planning, strategy and logic
- Answers need to be very clear and precise
- Memorise the CPS Code key areas
- Differentiate clearly between the evidential and public interest tests.

❝ What is the main role and function of the CPS? Discuss. ❞

❝ Outline the main factors that constitute the sufficient evidence criteria, followed by the factors that constitute the public interest test (criteria) for the CPS to review its cases. Discuss with reference to the CPS Code why the prosecution may decide to discontinue a case. ❞

To answer these questions well, you need to be factually correct in your answers. Apply the Code and its two-part test (see www.cps.gov.uk). Give reasons why a prosecution of an accused may not go ahead (e.g. not enough evidence by police; suspect is too old or sick; if convicted the likely outcome might only be a small fine etc).

Taking it **FURTHER**

1. With regards to the *Guildford Four*, you may wish to undertake further legal research into this case, see: *R v Hill and others*, *The Times*, 23 October 1975, p. 1; *The Times*, 28 February 1977, p. 2; *The Times*, 20 October 1989; Lords Devlin and Scarman, 'Justice and the Guildford Four' (1988) *The Times*, 30 November 1988, p. 16; Scrivener, 1989, 'The Guildford Four'; Logan, 1994, 'In the name of the father' (movie).

2. Read the 'May Report' (1993) by Sir John May. A Report of the inquiry into the circumstances surrounding the convictions arising out of the bomb attacks in Guildford and Woolwich in 1974.

3. Look up *R v McIlkenny* [1992] 93 Cr App Rep 287.

4. Read and comment on the famous judgement by Lloyd LJ in the Court of Appeal – Criminal Division (CA) in the *Birmingham Six* case, whereby the appellants had been convicted in 1975 of 21 counts of murder, arising out of the IRA bombing of two pubs in Birmingham.

Textbook guide

MANSFIELD, M. (1993*) Presumed Guilty. London: Heinemann*.

SLAPPER, G. AND KELLY, D. (2004) *Chapter 10 'The Criminal Process: Prosecution', in The English Legal System. 7th ed. London: Cavendish.*

WALKER, C. AND STARMER, K. (1999) *Miscarriages of Justice: A Review of Justice in Error. London: Blackstone Press.*

2.6

the magistrates' court

This section explains the workings of the Magistrates' Court (MC) and its main functionaries. There are currently about 30,000 'ordinary' members of the public as lay Magistrates who give up at least 52 days a year to serve – unremunerated – as Justices of the Peace (JP) in the local criminal courts. This section highlights what is meant by 'mode of trial' and bail decisions. Furthermore, this section provides you with practical issues on sentencing procedures. At the end of this section, you will be skilled at distinguishing between 'summary', 'either-way' and 'indictable' offences, and how these are dealt with in the MCs under new powers of the *Criminal Justice Act 2003*.

Core areas: **Tasks and powers of the Magistrates' Courts**

Who are the Magistrates?

Types of offences (summary, either-way, indictable)

Mode of trial: indication of plea

Bail decisions

Sentencing

The future of the magistracy.

Learning outcomes

By the end of this section you should be able to:

- Identify and explain the role and purpose of a Magistrates' Court (MC)
- Describe the roles played by all functionaries in the MC
- Recognise Modes of Trial decisions
- Give an explanation of 'Plea Before Venue'
- Give details and justify Magistrates' bail decisions.

Running themes

- Human rights
- Punishment
- Victims of crime
- Inequality
- Crime and the media.

Tasks and powers of the Magistrates' Courts

Nearly all criminal cases (about 95%) are heard in the Magistrates' Courts (MC) today, with the exception of violent and serious offences, known as *indictable* offences (e.g. murder, rape, or s 18 OAPA 1861(GBH with intent)). The age when a person can become a Magistrate (Justice of the Peace – JP) has been lowered to 18, in order to attract more young people on to the Bench. Generally speaking, Magistrates are older with retirement usually around 70, though in practice, many Benches still have to use retired JPs because they are so short staffed (especially the Greater London Courts Authority).

Who are the Magistrates?

For over 600 years, Justices of the Peace (JPs) have undertaken the greater part of the judicial work carried out in England and Wales. Magistrates are members of the local community appointed by the Lord Chancellor (Department of Constitutional Affairs – DCA). No formal qualifications are required, but JPs need intelligence, common sense, integrity and the capacity to act fairly. Membership should be widely spread throughout the area covered and drawn from all walks of life.

The DCA's main aim is to recruit suitable candidates from the ethnic minorities, proportionally from the areas for which they are responsible: today's Magistrates ought to reflect the profile of the neighbourhood they live in. The voting pattern and political views should be broadly reflected in the composition of the Bench and there should be no more than 15% of JPs on a Bench from the same occupational group. All Magistrates are carefully trained and appraised throughout their service.

Apart from Magistrates, there are about 130 *District Judges* (DJs) who operate mostly in London and greater metropolitan areas. DJs have at least seven years experience as a Barrister or Solicitor and two years experience as a Deputy District Judge. They sit alone and deal with more complex or sensitive cases (e.g. cases arising from the *Extradition Act 2003* or the *Fugitive Offenders Act 1967*. Until August 2000 these DJs were known as 'Stipendiary Magistrates', but were renamed in order to recognise them as members of the professional judiciary.

Features of a Magistrates' Court

Magistrates' Bench
Usually three Justices of the Peace (JPs) will sit, of mixed sex and ethnic background. A single 'Magistrate' will sit: this means a *District Judge* (i.e. professionally qualified lawyer – formerly 'Stipendiary Magistrate').

Legal Advisor's Bench
(Formerly: Justice's Clerk)
Trained lawyer who will sit in front of the Magistrates and explain the law to the justices.

Defence solicitor and CPS
Both the prosecutor (CPS) and the defence solicitor (sometimes a barrister) will sit across the room, side by side.

Dock
Defendant(s) will be placed in the dock during the hearings or trial (sometimes behind glass).

Probation Desk
Normally sit at the side of the court. A Probation Officer provides a Pre-Sentence Report (PSR) or Special Sentence Report (SSR) on the defendant to help the Magistrates on sentencing.

Witness Box
This is for the giving of evidence to the court. There will be a number of holy books for the judicial oath.

Press
Not normally present in court unless the case is newsworthy.

Public Gallery
Anyone can sit in court and hear the case (open justice principle), unless the court is sitting *in camera* (e.g. with juvenile cases in the Youth Court or family proceedings).

Types of offences

There are *three* main broad categories of criminal offences. Statute now determines most offence types; this in turn will determine where the case is to be heard – either in the Magistrates' Court or the Crown Court before judge and jury.

Types of offences

1 Indictable offences

2 Summary offences

3 Offences triable-either-way (either-way offence)

Magistrates deal with two categories of crime:

- *Summary* offences (less serious e.g. driving offences, harassment)
- *Either-way* offences (more serious e.g. theft, assault).

Summary offences

- *Less serious offences (s 40 CJA 1988)*
- *Adults (over 18) are tried 'summarily' (Interpretation Act 1978, Sch 1)*
- *Tried in Magistrates' Court*
- *Most summary offences are statutory.*

An example of an *indictable* offence is murder. No matter how serious the charge, the defendant has to appear first before Magistrates, where he confirms his name and address, and the legal advisor (formerly 'clerk to the justices') reads out the charge. Magistrates will then commit the defendant to the Crown Court. This happened with the school caretaker Ian Huntley, charged with the murder of the two 10-year-old Soham girls, Holly Wells and Jessica Chapman, in September 2002. Once charged, he first appeared in front of Peterborough MC, to confirm his name and address; the Bench then committed him for trial *on indictment* to the Crown Court. The 'Soham Trial' took place at the Central Criminal Court (The Old Bailey) in London between October and December 2003. Huntley was found guilty on two counts of murder and sentenced to life imprisonment.

Indictable offences

- *Serious offences in statute (e.g. grievous bodily harm with intent (GBH) s 18* Offences Against the Person Act 1861 *(OAPA); robbery – s 8* Theft Act 1968*)*
- *Serious sexual offences (e.g. rape;* Sexual Offences Act 2003*)*
- *Serious common law offences (e.g. homicide – murder/manslaughter)*
- *Any offence punishable by long or life imprisonment*
- *Only adults (over 18) are tried 'on indictment'*
- *Trial at Crown Court (judge and jury).*

Triable-either-way offences

- *Offence can be tried 'either way' (Magistrates' or Crown Court)*
- *Defendant (over 18) chooses whether he wants to be tried summarily (Magistrates) or on indictment (Crown Court, judge and jury)*
- *Statute prescribes 'either way' offences (e.g. 'Criminal Damage' – s 1* Criminal Damage Act 1971; *'making off without payment' – s 3* Theft Act 1978; *'assault occasioning actual bodily harm' (ABH) – s 47 OAPA).*

Where the accused (defendant) has a choice of *trial on indictment* (judge and jury in Crown Court), or *summary trial* (Magistrates), the following points ought to be born in mind:

- *Summary trial* is less time consuming
- Early guilty pleas must be reflected in defendant's sentence (e.g. lesser costs, lighter sentence)
- Punishment by Magistrates must not exceed £5000 (Level 5 fine) or six months' imprisonment
- Trial by jury (*on indictment*) offers better prospect of acquittal
- Jurors more likely to believe the accused (Magistrates less gullible and case hardened)
- *Disclosure*: defence knows prosecution's evidence (*CPIA 1996*)
- Crown Court judge decides on admissible evidence (in jury's absence).

The most interesting yet tricky category of crimes are *triable-either-way* offences. If the accused is charged with an 'either-way' offence, the prosecution must provide the Bench with advice as to where the case should be heard (e.g. 'the CPS advises that this case can be heard in the Magistrates' Court').

Magistrates have to consider the following criteria when deciding whether the either-way offence is to be tried summarily (MC) or on indictment (Crown Court):

- Nature and seriousness of the offence
- Is the punishment (sentencing) power of the MC adequate enough?
- Are there any other circumstances which make it more suitable for Crown Court?
- What are the representations by the prosecution?

> **Common pitfalls:** Make sure you don't confuse the various offence-types and be aware of the significance of triable-either-way offences, which affect mode of trial decisions by justices. This depends on the types of offences and the criminal charges laid by the CPS.

Mode of trial: indication of plea

It is at the MC where Mode of Trial decisions are decided. This is most crucial in *triable-either-way* offences.

> *Mode of trial (summary or on indictment)*
>
> - *Bench considers seriousness of offence (e.g. burglary in an occupied dwelling or unoccupied warehouse?)*
> - *Are Magistrates' sentencing powers sufficient in this case?*
> - *Is offence so serious that only custody will suffice?*
> - *Is discharge or a fine appropriate?*
> - *Any aggravating or mitigating factors? (e.g. Was there a forcible entry? Were victims injured? Vulnerable victims? Large damage? etc).*

*Plea Before Venue (PBV) and mode
of trial – a structured approach*

The following diagram should help you understand mode of trial and committal proceedings in the Magistrates' Court and explains the structured approach to Plea Before Venue (PBV).

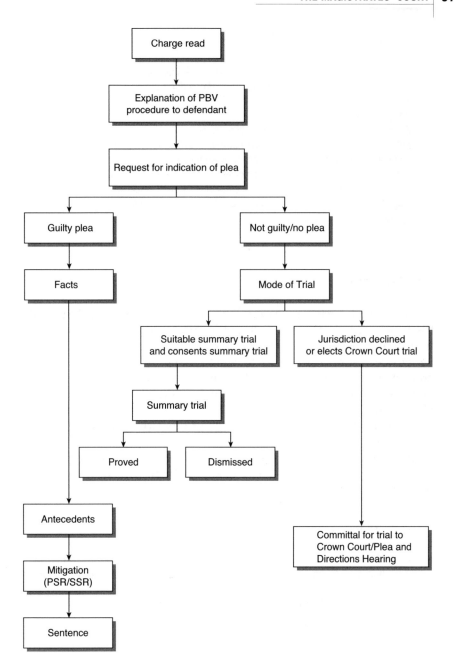

Common pitfalls:

- If you are not sure what type of offence you are dealing with, have a look at the prescribed statute (e.g. *Theft Act 1968, Protection from Harassment Act 1997* etc)
- Don't rely on guesswork
- Watch out for offences which are *triable-either-way*
- *Either-way* offences are generally tried *summarily* (Magistrates)
- If you are faced with a problem question as to mode of trial decision, you will usually find that where a case involves *complex questions of fact* or difficult *questions of law* (such as issues of disclosure of sensitive material), Magistrates will usually and decline jurisdiction decide on committal for trial to the Crown Court (*on indictment*).

Bail decisions

During a bail decision hearing, the prosecution (CPS) will provide the Bench with details of the alleged offence/s and any previous convictions (antecedents). The CPS will make their representations as to bail, i.e. advise the Magistrates as to whether they should or should not grant bail or remand the defendant in custody. The defence then provides details of the defence version of the allegations, the defendant's circumstances and their presentations as to bail. The court has to listen to all representations, but can ask questions (which makes this part *inquisitorial*).

Since incoming **human rights** legislation, Magistrates are duty-bound to apply the *Human Rights Act 1998* strictly in all parts of the criminal procedure. The following are the most relevant:

- Art. 5 ECHR – 'Right to liberty and security' (e.g. adequate time for defence)
- Art. 6 ECHR – 'Right to a fair trial' (e.g. fair and public hearing; reasonable time allocation for cases; independent and impartial tribunal; presumption of innocence)
- Art. 8 ECHR – 'Right to respect for private and family life'.

On granting bail with conditions (or not), Magistrates must explain the purpose of imposing conditions under human rights legislation, and give specific reasons for applying these conditions (equally when remanding in custody).

Bail Decisions

- *The defendant has the right to* unconditional bail
- Unconditional bail: *defendant has* prima facie *right to be 'free' whilst investigations into his case are ongoing*
- Conditional bail – *court will allow defendant to be 'free' with conditions (e.g. reside at certain address; must not interfere with witnesses; must report to police station; door-step curfew; electronic tagging etc)*
- *Bail* not *granted when defendant charged with homicide (murder; attempted murder; manslaughter) or rape or attempted rape*
- Remand in custody – *no bail is granted (prison).*

No bail *is granted if defendant*

- *Fails to surrender to custody*
- *Commits further offences whilst on bail*
- *Interferes with witness/es*
- *Obstructs the course of justice*
- *Has previously breached bail conditions*
- *Is already in custody*
- *Poses significant risk to public security (s 14 CJA 2003, amending Sch. 1 of* Bail Act 1976*)*
- *For defendant's own protection (police informer; suicidal; famous criminal).*

Sentencing

The fact that an offender has admitted his or her guilt does not make the offence itself any less serious … neither is it strictly a matter of personal mitigation, on a par with the offender's state of health or family circumstances. (*Sentencing Advisory Panel Guidelines 2003*)

Sentencing in the Magistrates' Courts

- *Magistrates have limited sentencing powers (Crown Court has unlimited sentencing powers)*
- *Magistrates must take early guilty pleas into account upon sentencing*
- *'Community Sentence' must be considered before considering custody*
- *'Sufficiently serious' test must be applied in each case*
- *Risk assessment of offender (of future risk or harm to society) must be applied (low, medium, high).*

Prison sentences (CJA 2003)

- All sentences *below 12 months* must have a minimum term of 28 weeks
- The 28 weeks should be made up of: two-week 'custodial period' + 26-week 'licence period' (*custody plus*)
- *Intermittent custody* – weekend or evening imprisonment
- Courts have to consider the seriousness of the offence
- Courts have to consider the offender's culpability in committing the offence, and
- Any harm which the offence caused
- Courts have to apply the 'sufficiently serious-test'; this includes
- Considering the seriousness of the (current) offence committed by the offender; and
- His previous convictions (antecedents) if relevant to current offence
- Only sufficiently serious offences merit prison (at least 6 months).

The future of the magistracy

The *Auld Report* (2001) pointed to a disjointed system of in-fighting between police, CPS, other agencies and governmental departments (Home Office). This meant that at least half of all criminal cases brought to the CPS collapsed by 1997. Auld recommended a 'professionalisation' of the magistracy that could not always deliver an efficient and speedy system. Reading between the lines, Auld advised to abandon the lay magistracy and only employ professional (District) judges.

Is there a future for the lay magistracy? Arguably, the professionally qualified lawyer would undertake a far greater role, but on the other hand, the lay magistracy is more representative of 'the people' (and certainly cheaper than employing full-time District Judges). The Government has decided to keep the lay magistracy for the time being, because this gives society a democratic representativeness, and has taken the view that the lay magistracy is perfectly able to undertake the work that it currently performs but that the training should be, and is being improved. Furthermore, the focus should be more on the professional rather than the 'lay' and the Department for Constitutional Affairs (DCA) is currently examining 'fast tracking' legally qualified Magistrates, to sit alone on the Bench.

The following are test yourself-type self-reflective questions that require short answers (about 300 words):

"How are criminal procedures initiated?"

Start with arrest by the police and how the CPS then lays the charges.

"Who makes a triable-either-way decision?"

Describe and define either-way offences; discuss defendant's choice where his case may be heard (Magistrates' vs. Crown Court). Discuss issues in favour of the defendant choosing trial by Magistrates.

"What is meant by Conditional Bail? Give examples."

Where court imposes certain conditions on the defendant e.g. doorstep curfew; presenting himself to the local police station; not to contact witnesses etc.

"What is meant by Unconditional Bail? Give examples."

The defendant is 'free' to leave the police station/court but must present himself at the next dated hearing at court. Give examples why there might be no bail conditions on the defendant (e.g. minor offence; first-time offender).

"What is meant by an 'early guilty' plea?"

The defendant pleads guilty at the Magistrates' Court to an alleged offence; Magistrates move straight to sentencing (e.g. motoring offence, such as drink-driving – driving with excess alcohol etc); the defendant is entitled to a reduction in sentence.

"What does 'remand in custody' mean?"

The defendant is refused bail; give reasons why bail might be refused by Magistrates (e.g. serious imprisonable offence; antecedents of (re)offending whilst on bail; interference with witnesses.

To answer the above questions successfully, you need to read up on:

- Prosecution and the CPS
- The evidential test and the public interest test
- Pre-trial procedure

- Pleading guilty or not guilty (Plea Before Venue)
- Modes of trial (summary; indictable; either-way offences)
- Remand or bail
- *Human Rights Act 1998* and Magistrates' Courts Act 1980.

Here follow some longer 'essay-type' questions. Write at least two sides of A4 on each question:

"What are the advantages and disadvantages of the lay Magistracy?"

Describe what is meant by 'lay' (non-lawyers); explain the unique English system that Magistrates try about 97% of all criminal cases. Argue their objectivity and who can become a Magistrate. Address social background, ethnicity, race etc. Negative aspects might be that case-loads take longer than being tried by one (legally trained) District Judge. Look at Lord Justice Auld's Review of the Criminal Courts and his recommendation regarding the future of the magistracy (abolition in favour of full-time paid judges). But what about the costs?

"What criteria are used by Magistrates during bail decisions?"

Describe adversarial justice system, but also the point where the inquisitorial process takes place (bail decision). JPs look at nature of the alleged offence; any antecedents (bad character – CJA 2003); and listen to representations by prosecution and defence. Impact of *Human Rights Act 1998*. Discuss defendant's fundamental right to bail.

Taking it **FURTHER**

1. What, in your opinion, is the implication of the notion that people are 'innocent until proven guilty' in the light of recent changes with the *Criminal Justice Act* (CJA) *2003* (e.g. introduction of 'bad character' or the abolition of the doctrine of double jeopardy)?
2. What were the improvements made post *Auld Report* (Lord Justice Auld 'Review of the Criminal Courts in England and Wales', 2001: to process adult offenders through the criminal courts more speedily? Consult the *Powers of Criminal Courts [Sentencing] Act 2000* and the CJA 2003.

You may wish to study some case law:

3. *R v Savage*; *R v Parmenter* – both judgements on same day [1992] 1 AC 699 [HL]; [1991] 4 All ER 698 – *Savage*: 'assault' (ABH–s 20 OAPA 1861) by throwing a pint of beer on victim? *Parmenter*: 'assault' by inflicting injuries on baby whilst 'playing with him vigorously'?
4. *R v Ireland* (Robert Matthew); *R v Burstow* (Anthony Christopher) – both judgements on same day 1997 AC 147; [1997] 3 WLR 534 – *Ireland*: stalking by silent, anonymous telephone calls; *Burstow*: can unwanted stroking or kissing amount to 'assault'?
5. *R v Marcus* [1981] 2 All ER 833 (CA) – administering sleeping tablets to someone whom you just want to annoy.

Textbook guide

ASHWORTH, A. AND REDMAYNE, M. (2005) *The Criminal Process*. 3rd ed. Oxford: OUP.

GIBSON, B. AND WATKINS, M. (2004) *Criminal Justice Act 2003: a guide to the new procedures and sentencing*. Winchester: Waterside Press.

GROVE, T. (2003) *The Magistrate's Tale: a front line report from a new JP*. London: Bloomsbury.

MITCHELL, B. AND FARRAR, S. (2005) *Blackstone's Statutes on Criminal Justice and Sentencing* 2nd ed. Oxford: OUP.

2.7	
the crown court	

Her Majesty's Crown Court is part of the Supreme Court of Judicature of England and Wales – alongside the High Court of Justice and the Court of Appeal. The Crown Court is a permanent unitary court across England and Wales – a kind of 'Higher Court of First Instance' in all serious criminal cases. The most famous Crown Court is the 'Central Criminal Court' in London, better known as 'The Old Bailey'.

Core areas: **Functions of the Crown Court**
                   Juries and their role
                   Jury and witness intimidation
                   The verdict.

Learning outcomes

By the end of this section you should be able to:

- Give a general overview of the English court system
- Have detailed knowledge of the main functionaries in the criminal courts
- Understand the main functions of the Crown Court
- Show detailed knowledge of the type of offences
- Identify the role and function of a Crown Court jury.

Running themes

- Human rights
- Punishment
- Inequality
- Race
- Gender.

Functions of the Crown Court

The Crown Court was established in 1972 by the *Courts Act 1971;* many of its decisions have now been repealed by the *Supreme Court Act 1981.* The Crown Court hears *indictable-only* offences, and those 'either-way' offences which Magistrates have committed to the Crown Court because they feel their sentencing powers aren't adequate enough, or the defendant himself has chosen Crown Court trial by judge and jury. Crown Court trials are heard by a judge and a 12-person jury. Apart from people actually involved in the cases, members of the public may have to go to court as witnesses or to do jury service. The Crown sits in 78 locations in England and Wales and deals with more serious criminal cases transferred from the Magistrates' Court such as:

- Murder
- Rape
- Robbery.

The Crown Court also hears appeals against decisions made in the Magistrates' Courts and deals with cases sent from Magistrates' Courts for sentence.

The trial will usually progress as follows:

- *Counsel for the prosecution opens his case*
- *Witnesses for the prosecution*
- *Counsel for the defence may open his case*
- *Witnesses for the defence*
- *Counsel for the prosecution sums up his case*
- *Counsel for the defence sums up the case for the defence*
- *Summing up to the jury by the judge*
- *Jury retire and return with verdict.*

Juries and their role

> We believe that twelve persons selected at random are likely to be a cross-selection of the people as a whole and thus represent the views of the common man. (Lord Denning MR in *R v Sheffield Crown Court ex parte Brownlow* [1980]).

Crown Court trials are heard by a jury of 12 people and a judge. Around 500,000 jurors are selected at random by computer every year and are called to listen to the evidence and give their verdict of guilty or not guilty. Jury service is a public duty that members of the public must perform, if selected. Most juries are selected to try crimes but juries are also used in Coroner's inquests and in some civil cases (e.g. defamation or 'libel' actions in the High Court). A jury at Leeds Crown Court in the Harold Shipman inquest, for instance, returned a verdict of suicide on 22 April 2005 after a ten-day hearing at Leeds Crown Court. Shipman was found hanged in his cell in Wakefield Prison on 13 January 2004, a day before his 58th birthday. He had been convicted in 2000 for murdering 15 patients but is thought to have killed a further 235.

Criminal Court Structure

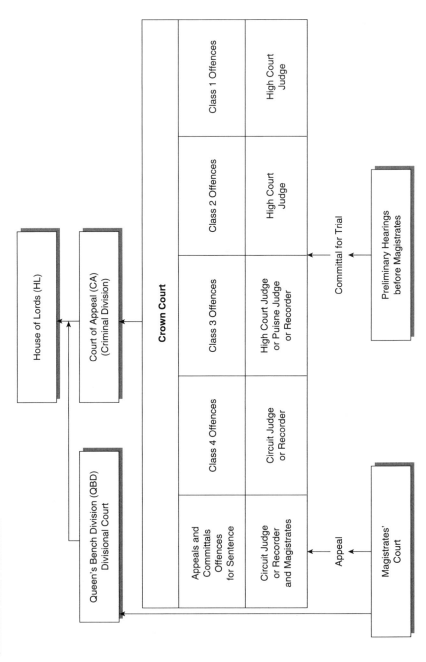

The functions of a jury in criminal cases

- *Attend crown court about two weeks or duration of trial*
- *Try serious criminal cases*
- *Must weigh up evidence and decide on facts of case (i.e. what actually happened).*
- *Decide on 'guilty' or 'not guilty' of defendant.*

The CJA 2003 introduced some fundamental changes from 1 April 2005 in relation to jury service (based on recommendations in the *Auld Report*, 2001). The main aim was to greatly increase the pool of potential jurors needed for jury service each year. The Act has made jury service more or less compulsory for anyone summoned who is on the electoral register and has lived in the UK (including Magistrates).

Juries and the Criminal Justice Act 2003

- *Everyone* registered on the electoral roll aged 18–70 *must* serve on a jury if summoned
- Some of those who previously had a right to be excused from jury service are now *obliged* to serve as jurors (e.g. Peers; members of the medical professions; members of certain religious bodies)
- Members of certain professions such as the legal profession, police services and others who were previously disqualified from jury service *must* now serve as jurors (including Magistrates)

Jury and witness intimidation

Under the *Criminal Justice and Public Order Act 1994* it is an offence to intimidate a person whom the offender believes to be a potential or actual witness or juror. This is called 'jury intimidation' (also known as jury 'nobbling'), where someone involved in the trial puts pressure on jurors to vote in a particular way, by bribes or threats. It is a criminal offence to attempt to influence a jury's discussions or to question them about their discussions when the case is over. It is also a criminal offence to intimidate a juror in relation to proceedings with which he is connected (this falls under the 'contempt of court' legislation – *Contempt of Court Act 1981*).

The verdict

Ideally the verdict of a jury should be *unanimous*. In 1967 *majority verdicts* were introduced of 10 to 2 (or 9 to 1 if the jury has been reduced during the trial); i.e. when there are at least 10 people on the jury and they cannot reach a unanimous verdict, a majority verdict is acceptable. If found guilty, the accused will be punished (sentenced) on indictment. This is set by statute for most criminal offences or life imprisonment for a murder conviction. Crown Courts can set an unlimited fine.

❝ Describe and evaluate the jury system of England and Wales. What, in your opinion, are the advantages and disadvantages, and how has the system changed after the introduction of the CJA 2003? ❞

You need to describe the jury trial within the administration of justice in England and Wales and discuss the constitutional principle that no person should be imprisoned for a serious crime unless he has been found guilty by his peers. Briefly discuss other (civil) juries, but concentrate on the criminal process. You need to address the role of the judge and the fact that he must give a general direction to the jury. Juries find the defendant guilty/not guilty on the facts of the case presented to them. You need to discuss the standard and burden of proof and the importance of the judge's summing up; miscarriages of justice or a re-trial. Finally, you must address new legislation regarding jury service under the CJA 2003 and the proposed use of expert juries in serious fraud cases.

❝ What is the fundamental principle enshrined in English law as established by the case of *Woolmington v DPP* [1935]? ❞

Here you need to address the 'golden thread' theory of proof and the general principle, laid down in *Woolmington* that the burden is on the prosecution to prove the facts essential to their case. You also need to address exceptions to this general principle which are expressly stated in statute and place the legal burden on the accused (e.g. 'it shall be for the defendant to prove…'), or where on interpreting the statute, it implies that the burden is on the accused. Give examples.

Taking it ***FURTHER***

Look up and comment on the following cases:

1. *R v Sheffield Crown Court, ex parte Brownlow* [1980] QB 530 (CA) – Judicial Review case (*ex parte*) regarding jury vetting and previous convictions.
2. *R v Andrews* (Tracey) [1999] Crim LR 156 – High profile case where defendant was accused of murdering her boyfriend. Defence wanted to issue questionnaire to jury to establish prejudice.
3. *Gregory v UK* [1998] 25 EHRR 577 – European Court of Human Rights [ECHR] case where a juror was accused of racial bias.
4. *Sander v UK* [2001] 31 EHRR 44 – Allegations of racial bias towards an Asian defendant.
5. *Grobbelaar v News Group Newspapers Ltd* [2001] EWCA Civ 33 – Concerns jury bias in the high profile civil (libel) case of the former Liverpool FC goalkeeper, Bruce Grobbelaar, against the *Sun* newspaper for defamation.
6. *Sutcliffe v Pressdram Ltd* [1991] 1 QB 153 – Sonia Sutcliffe (wife of the 'Yorkshire Ripper' Peter Sutcliffe) took (civil) legal action against *Private Eye* in a civil (libel) action. Jury bias.

Textbook guide

ASHWORTH, A. AND REDMAYNE, M. (2005) *The Criminal Process.* 3rd ed. Oxford: OUP.'The Trial' (Ch. 11); 'Appeals' (Ch. 12).

ELLIOTT, C. AND QUINN, F. (2005) *English Legal System,* 5th ed. London: Longman-Pearson. Parts 2 and 3: 'The jury system' (Ch. 12); 'Magistrates' (Ch. 13); 'Human Rights' (Ch. 15).

ZANDER, M. (1999) *The Law Making Process.* London: Butterworths.

2.8	
youth crime and youth justice	

This section begins by giving the reader a brief insight into criminological research, based on psychological theories that dysfunctional elements in family set-ups can be central to deviant or criminal behaviour in youngsters. From the age of 10–17, young people appear in the Youth Court (usually a part of the Magistrates' Court) and are dealt with by specially trained Magistrates. This makes England one of the most punitive countries in the world, with one of the lowest ages of criminal responsibility. Proceedings may be reported in the press but the young person may not generally be identified (*Children and Young Persons Act 1933*).

The section also includes an overview of youth justice policies and how persistent young offenders have been punished over the past decade. Since 1997, anti-social behaviour legislation has been at the forefront of governmental penal policy (*Crime and Disorder Act 1998*) and terminology now includes: lager louts; football hooligans; mobile phone thieves; and joy-riders.

Core areas: **Young people and crime**

Level of youth crime

Youth justice policies

The Youth Justice Board (YJB)

Youth Offending Teams (YOTs)

Youth Courts

Sentencing young offenders

Young people in prison

Custodial sentences for young offenders.

Learning outcomes

By the end of this section you should be able to:

- Show awareness of youth justice legislation; and
- Show awareness of youth justice agencies in the English criminal justice system

- Characterise and quantify levels of youth crime in England/Wales
- Explain various youth sentencing options available to the courts; and
- Illustrate the use of Young Offender Institutions.

Running themes

- Inequality
- Gender
- Race
- Human rights
- Victims and crime
- Punishment
- Criminalisation
- Crime and the media.

Young people and crime

Youth studies have traditionally focused on subcultures, such as punks, skinheads and the dance culture, and likened these phenomena to **inequality** and inner-city deprivation (see Hall and Jefferson, 1976). The notion of **criminalisation** and economic deprivation refers to the perception of being deprived of something (e.g. a good career, consumer goods etc) – which *may* lead young people to commit crime. However, research found that not all deprived youngsters turn to crime. On the contrary, certain boys and girls are well integrated into society, because they have developed tough resilient identities, with expressions of intelligence or smartness.

One term you will come across in this context is anomie. This concept, first defined by the French Sociologist Émile Durkheim, established the idea that when people find themselves in rapidly changing social conditions, they will lose the social guidelines or *norms* to their behaviour. Durkheim saw anomie, for instance, resulting from the transition of a rural agrarian society into an urban one; this leads to a state of *normlessness* and a lack of understanding of acceptable behaviours. He explained his ideas in his book *The Division of Labour in Society* (1893). Durkheim also researched suicide as a way to show the results of anomie. He was able to demonstrate that suicide rates increased when economic conditions declined. He then hypothesised that social change in conditions could create a state of anomie and lead to an increase in suicide rates (see his *Suicide: A Study in Sociology*, 1897). He further believed that crime was a natural consequence and a 'normal' part of society.

Causes of youth crime (criminogenic factors)

- *Deviant and criminal behaviour tends to be influenced by societal and familial factors*
- *Criminologists and social scientists strongly believe that deviance and criminality are never solely founded on biological factors, but*
- Criminogenic *factors depend on interaction of the social and familial background of a child*
- *Causes of crime are largely linked to life-style, life-cycle and familial conditions in which a youngster is raised*
- *To change criminogenic factors and deviant behaviour the child's present environment and life-style have to change dramatically to make a difference.*

What, then, are the causes of deviance, anomie and youth crime? Muncie (2004) notes that one of the overwhelming causes of deviant and criminal behaviour is an increase in gang and bohemian youth culture, and the fundamental collapse of norms and traditional social values. Such a decline in non-conformist youth cultures, he argues, has led to subcultures, deviant drug-taking and extensive illicit use of alcohol. Areas with little employment for school leavers and immense school exclusion will show a propensity in criminality where subjects of 'earning' pleasure and adherence to cultural norms simply do not exist, since criminal opportunities are largely undertaken in the youngsters' own close social field, such as large council estates. There are other issues surrounding youth crime, such as **racism** and the urban multiculture.

Key thinkers

- **Émile Durkheim** (1858–1917) born in Épinal, France. Social and political Philosopher. His work is related to *Functionalism*, i.e. he examined social differentiation as part of a scientific method to study modern society. His *Anomie Theory* (normlessness) marked the boundaries of acceptable and unacceptable behaviour and social norms set by society. He strongly believed that some level of *deviance* was normal and functional in society.

- **John E. Bowlby** (1907–90) British Psychoanalyst famous for his work on the early separation of an infant from his mother, posing a biological attachment need to explain both the infant's immediate responses, and later adult behaviour (so-called 'attachment theory'). His work, whilst controversial amongst feminists, was influential in changing practices in nurseries and children's wards in hospitals. See Bowlby (1979) *The Making and Breaking of Affectional Bonds*, and Bowlby (1988) *Secure Base*.
- **Charles Murray** (1943–) Social Scientist, born and raised in Newton, Iowa. He has undertaken extensive research into familial background, single parent families and *inequality* and *crime* (the 'creation of the underclass'). He compares a child's development in line with maternal vs. paternal deprivation and blames fatherless families for the emergence of an 'underclass' society. The term 'underclass' suggests a group that is in some sense outside the mainstream of society – but there is much disagreement about the nature and source of their exclusion. One interpretation, advanced by Murray, is that welfare dependency has encouraged the break-up of the *nuclear family* household, and socialisation into a *counter-culture*, which devalues work and encourages dependency and criminality. Murray argues that the ambitious social programmes of the 'Great Societies' (e.g. Britain or the USA), designed to help the poor and disadvantaged not only did not accomplish what they set out to do, but also often made things worse. See Murray (1984) *Losing Ground: American Social Policy 1950–1980*.

Common pitfalls: Here are some general hints on how to tackle a discursive essay regarding youth crime, causes of crime and juvenile delinquency:

- *Don't generalise: not all youngsters from deprived or disadvantaged backgrounds turn to crime*
- *Children can develop positive capabilities and survival mechanisms even if they grow up in dysfunctional families*
- *Youngsters can 'iron out' (overcome) their unfavourable social familial background, by attaching themselves to other 'social agents' (friends, neighbours, teachers)*
- *Inherited familial behaviour patterns can be simply accepted but not necessarily upheld or followed socially*
- *Children from severely dysfunctional families do not always show any signs of deviant or criminal behaviour; but*
- *Some do show psychological disturbance patterns which can be particularly prevalent in girls (**gender** and **crime**)*
- *Some forms of family 'disorder' (dysfunctionality) has proven to influence certain criminal behaviour or deviance patterns.*

Level of youth crime

The criminal law of England and Wales today states that children under the age of 10 cannot commit crimes. It is felt that on the whole, children under 10 are too young to weigh up what is right and wrong and to deliberately break the law. When very young children get into serious trouble, or they have problems, social workers often try to help them and their families but if children are out of control, a Youth Court can have them taken into care. When children reach the age of 10, they can be arrested and charged with crimes and taken to court in the same way as adults can, depending on the crime.

Nearly a quarter of people (22%) canvassed by the British Crime Survey (2004) perceived a high level of disorder and juvenile offending in their local area. One in three people (33%) cited teenagers 'hanging around' on the streets as the biggest problem.

Youth crime statistics

- About seven million offences are committed by under 18s each year
- The mean age of offending for boys is 18–21 and for girls, 15
- Girls seem to grow out of crime quicker than boys
- Children can go to prison from age 12 (Young Offender Institutions – HMYOIs).

Youth justice policies

Reducing youth crime and reforming the youth justice system became a major part of the New Labour Government's efforts to build safer communities and tackle **inequality** and social exclusion from 1997 onwards. The *Crime and Disorder Act 1998* introduced 'Anti-Social Behaviour Orders' (ASBOs) to exclude young deviants from certain areas where they have terrorised their neighbourhoods. Now widely used by local authorities, these civil actions can be imposed by either courts or local authorities in order to combat crime and to restrict young offenders' movements in a particular area.

Crime and Disorder Act 1998 (CDA)

- Governmental strategy re. prevention of persistent re-offending by children and young people
- Aim: to prevent persistent youth offending

- Creates statutory duty on all those working in the youth justice system
- Provides early interventions and punishments (YOTs)
- Strategies to help youthful offenders (and their parents) to face up to their offending behaviour and take responsibility for it
- Involves local communities and youth justice agencies
- New sentencing initiatives to 'crack down' on young offenders and their parents.

The Youth Justice Board

The Youth Justice Board (YJB) for England and Wales came into force on 30 September 1998 (s 41 CDA 1998). It oversees the operational side of local Youth Offending Teams (YOTs), and the youth justice system as a whole. It is a non-departmental public body, sponsored by the Home Office. The YJB consists of between 10 and 12 members appointed by the Home Secretary, including people who have extensive recent experience of the youth justice system. Since April 2000, the YJB has been responsible for commissioning places for children and young people remanded and sentenced by the courts to secure facilities. The YJB sets clear national targets within a framework thus leading the developing policy in youth justice. It also monitors the 155 YOTs; these in turn are locally accountable to both Criminal Justice and children's services.

Functions of the Youth Justice Board (YJB)

- **Monitors operation of youth justice system and provision of youth justice services**
- **Advises Home Secretary on setting of national standards for provision of youth justice services (YOTs and Youth Courts) and Young Offender Institutions (HMYOIs – custodial accommodation)**
- **Advises on how principal aim of youth justice system is most effectively pursued**
- **Identifies and promotes grants for development of good practice in operation of youth justice system and crime prevention**
- **Purchases and commissions places in secure and custodial institutions**
- **Allocates juvenile prisoners to HMYOIs.**

In summary, the YJB sees to the swift administration of justice and ensures that young people face up to the consequences of their offending. Through its Youth Offending Teams (YOTs) the Board further ensures that risk factors associated with youthful offending are addressed by early intervention. Any form of punishment should be proportionate to the seriousness and frequency of offending ('just deserts' philosophy) and young offenders should be encouraged at all times by the various agencies (YOTs, Youth Courts etc) to address the reparation of their crime to their victims (restorative justice; victim-offender mediation). Parental responsibility must be encouraged at all times.

Youth Offending Teams (YOTS)

Since 1 April 2000, Youth Offending Teams (YOTs) have been operational. YOTs are made up of social workers, police officers, probation officers, education and health staff, with the scope to involve others, including the voluntary sector. The function of YOTs involve:

- Support work of police with reprimands and warnings
- Supervise community sentences
- Ensure an 'appropriate adult' service (e.g. accompany children to court)
- Provide bail information; bail supervision and support
- Provide remand fostering and approved lodgings during pre-trial period
- Prepare court reports
- Involved in through-care (end-to-end offender management)
- Undertake post-release supervision following custodial sentence.

Youth Courts

Since the *Children and Young Persons Act 1933*, Magistrates, with special qualifications for this work, are elected by their colleagues in each Magistrates' Courts area or region to perform 'juvenile justice' functions. The *Youth Court* was introduced from 1 October 1992 and replaced 'Juvenile Courts'. In Youth Courts, no person is allowed to be present unless authorised by the court (*in camera*), except for the members and officers of the court, parties to the case (normally including parents/guardians), their legal representatives, witnesses and *bona fide* representatives of the **media** (s 39 *Children and Young Persons Act 1933*).

A child or young person (10–17) is generally tried in the Youth Court unless any of the following apply:

- *They are charged with homicide (e.g. murder or manslaughter); they must be sent to the Crown Court for trial*

- *They are aged 14+ and charged with a 'grave crime' ('adult' in nature; could be imprisoned for at least 14 years; indecent assault; rape; dangerous driving)*
- *They are charged jointly with adult (over 18) on 'grave' offence; both should be dealt with at Crown Court.*

Sentencing young offenders

In all Youth Court areas there are now fast track schemes in operation to facilitate speedy youth justice, covering 95% of persistent young offenders.

Legislation and punishment measures for young offenders

- Extended powers to the police (under PACE) to remove truants from premises (such as shopping centres) allow the police, working with local authorities and schools, to tackle truancy, one of the factors that put young people at risk of offending
- *Anti-Social Behaviour Orders* (ASBOs) Civil measures aimed to protect the public from behaviour that causes or is likely to cause harassment, alarm or distress; enforceable by local councils (s 1 *Crime and Disorder Act 1998*)
- *Parenting Orders* help reinforce and support parental responsibility (a parenting order may also be used in combination with an anti-social behaviour order or a child safety order)
- *Intensive Supervision and Surveillance Programmes* Introduced in 2001, aimed at dealing with persistent young offenders. Administered by the YJB
- *Satellite Tracking* – Monitors offenders' movements and ensures compliance with restrictions placed on them (e.g. ASBOs). Allows an offender to be monitored retrospectively with location data being downloaded at appropriate times for those considered 'high risk'.

The CDA 1998 introduced the following measures available to Youth Courts since 1 April 2000.

Reprimands and final warnings

The framework of the 'reprimand and final warning' scheme only applies to *under 18s* and replaces the old system of police cautions. Reprimands can be given to first-time offenders for *minor offences*. An assessment (by means of 'contract') usually involves contacting the **victim** to assess whether 'victim–offender mediation' or some form of restorative justice

(RJ) is appropriate. Any further offending results in either a final warning or a charge. The 'final warning' triggers immediate referral to a local YOT; they will assess the young person and, unless they consider it inappropriate, prepare a rehabilitation programme (or 'change' programme, as it is now known) designed to tackle the reasons for the young person's offending behaviour and to prevent any future offending.

Reprimands and final warnings

- *In the case of a first offence, police will decide, depending on the seriousness, to reprimand, give a final warning or prosecute*
- *Once a reprimand has been given, any further offence can only be dealt with by a final warning or charge*
- *Following a final warning, any other offences within two years will automatically result in criminal charges*
- *Whenever police issue a final warning they will refer the case to the YOT who will devise a programme of intervention for the child*
- *A reprimand or final warning cannot be given to anyone who has already been convicted of an offence.*

Measures to tackle anti-social behaviour

- Child curfews – *local schemes to 'protect' children under the age of 10 in a particular area from getting into trouble. Local authorities have power to apply to Home Secretary to establish local schemes under s 6 CDA 1998.*
- Child Curfew Orders and Child Safety Orders – *provide targeted intervention for children under 10 'at risk of getting into trouble'.*
- Child Curfews to the age of 15 – *allow police and local authorities to apply for extended curfew scheme under ss 48 and 49* Criminal Justice and Police Act 2001
- Anti-social Behaviour Orders (ASBOs) – *deal with serious, but not necessarily criminal, anti-social behaviour by children aged 10 and above (s 1 CDA 1998)*
- On the spot fines of £40 – *can be imposed by police on anyone (or their parents) who commits minor offences (e.g. insulting or abusive behaviour; making hoax 999-calls; drinking in a no-alcohol zone). Applies also to adults within* Anti-Social Behaviour Act 2003 *and extends fines to 16 and 17-year-olds.*

Non-custodial sentences

Where the Youth Court sees fit, all young offenders may be given *absolute* or *conditional* discharges. Young offenders aged 16+ may receive a *Probation*

Order or a Community Sentence (similar to adult court orders). Young offenders aged 10–17 may also be fined, but in certain cases their parent or guardian can be ordered to pay (parenting order).

Restorative justice (RJ) and the youth justice system (YJS)

- *YJS pioneered RJ since 1998*
- *YOTS offer 75% of victims of youth crime participation in RJ*
- *Mediation and conflict resolution between victim and offender*
- *Meeting with person they have harmed*
- *Community work where victim cannot (will not) be identified.*

There is now a wealth of *non-custodial sentences* in the form of orders. Under s 1 of the *Crime and Disorder Act 1998*, ASBOs were introduced to protect the public from 'harassment, alarm or distress' caused by (young) people. This meant that 'relevant authorities' (i.e. local authorities; police; British Transport Police; courts) can now apply for orders that prohibit an individual from specific anti-social or criminal acts. For instance, not entering defined areas, or entering certain buildings (e.g. wearing 'hoodies' or 'baseball caps' in shopping centres), leaving home after a certain time in the evening or prohibiting association with certain friends or acquaintances.

Anti-Social Behaviour Order (ASBO) (s 1 CDA 1998)

- Civil Order for any child aged 10 or over
- Breach of ASBO is criminal offence (punishable by a maximum of two years, custody)
- Order can prohibit any activity or entry into specified areas.

In February 2004, s 3 of the *Anti-Social Behaviour Act 2003* came into force, giving authorities further powers to punish parents of young people who truant, or behave very badly inside or outside school. Authorities can:

- Issue parents with a fixed penalty fine of £25–100 for their child's truancy; and
- Request a Parenting Order (see below)
- Ask court for an Anti-Social Behaviour Order for parents/guardians of pupils who misbehave
- Failure to comply with Parenting Order (criminal offence) results in a maximum of a £1000 fine.

Referral Order (Youth Justice and Criminal Evidence Act 1999)

- Offender referred to local Youth Offending Panel
- Mandatory sentence for most first-time defendants who plead guilty
- Contract agreed detailing the reparation and activities to be undertaken over a set period of time
- Failure to comply with contract results in return to Youth Court for re-sentencing (criminal offence).

Supervision Order

- Between three months and three years
- Young person supervised by YOT-Supervisor; or Probation (over 18); or local authority
- Contract: youth must agree 'specified activities' with Supervisor
- Victim-reparation Order (CDA 1998).

Attendance Centre Order

- Offender from aged 10 under 'supervision, appropriate occupation and instruction' (now up to 25-years-old – CJA 2003; under 18s maximum 12 hours)
- Requires offender to attend local centre for a maximum of three hours per day (usually Saturdays)
- Offender receives instruction on social skills and physical training.

Reparation Order (ss 67 and 68, CDA 1998)

- Requires an offender to make specified reparation to their victim (with victim's consent); or
- Non-financial reparation to victim or community at large (e.g. repairing damage caused by vandalism; graffiti removal; letter of apology)
- Can be imposed on anyone aged 10–17 who has committed an offence where the penalty is not fixed by law
- Reparation must be commensurate with the seriousness of the offence
- YOTs co-ordinate Reparation Orders
- Order *cannot* be combined with custodial sentence, or with a Community Service Order, a Combination Order, a Supervision Order or an Action Plan Order.

Action Plan Order (ss 69 and 70, CDA 1998)

- Provides short, intensive, individually tailored response to offending behaviour
- Specific programme of work designed to tackle offending behaviour (including Victim Reparation Order)

- Order lasts three months
- Youth Court can hold review hearing within two weeks of making order.

Parental Bind-Over Order

- For parents/guardians who have not exercised proper care and control over youngster
- Requires parents/guardians to exercise proper care and control over them
- Order specifies sum not exceeding £1000 (discretionary for 16 and 17-year-olds)
- Court must give reasons for not binding-over parents/guardians for youngsters under 16
- Period may not exceed three years (or until youngster is 18).

Parenting Order (ss 8 and 9, CDA 1998)

- Helps reinforce and support parental responsibilities
- Two elements: (1) requirement on the parent/guardian to attend counselling or guidance sessions – up to three months; (2) requirement encouraging parent/guardian to exercise a measure of control over the child (e.g. child must attend school; must avoid certain people or places) – up to 12 months
- For child under 16 convicted of an offence
- Adult must attend Parenting Skills course
- Order overseen by Probation Officer; Social Worker or YOT member.

Child Safety Order (s 11, CDA 1998)

- For child under 10 for up to three months; where
- Court feels the child is in danger of becoming involved in crime
- Supervising Officer or YOT member must ensure child is subject to appropriate support and control, and
- Must devise programmed activities.

Child Curfew Schemes (s 14, CDA 1998)

Though initially not used, local councils began to use local child curfew schemes during the hot summer of 2003 and more extensively from 2004 onwards (e.g. Avon, Bedfordshire, Cambridgeshire, Cleveland, Cumbria, Essex, Hampshire, Humberside, North Wales, Nottinghamshire, Somerset, South Wales, Surrey, Sussex, Warwickshire and West Mercia). This means that local police forces and local authorities have the power to pick up children aged under 16 who are outdoors after 9pm. Officers take them to their homes and require them, on the threat of a hefty fine or imprisonment, to stay there until 6am.

Young people in prison

Designated HMYOIs (Her Majesty's Young Offender Institutions) are:

Ashfield	Brinsford	Lancaster Farms	Thorn Cross
Castington	Feltham	Onley, Portland	Warrington
Hollesley Bay	Huntercombe	Stoke Heath	Wetherby

Though the HM Prison Service has endeavoured to improve regimes in Young Offender Institutions in order to take account of particular needs of adolescents, conditions in some HMYOIs remain intolerable and inhumane, contravening basic **human rights**. In March 2000 there were 2247 children in prison (including 87 girls). In 1993 the average sentence length was 8.6 months for boys and 6.9 months for girls. In 1999 it was 11.4 months for boys and 7.7 months for girls. During 1993, 4200 children were sentenced to immediate custody; by 1999 this figure had risen to 7000, an increase of 67%.

You may be asked to give reasons for the increase in the young prisoner population; here are some reasons you can advance:

- *Tougher sentencing legislation* (Crime and Disorder Act 1998; Youth Justice and Criminal Evidence Act 1999)
- *Increase in sentence lengths* (*The* Criminal Justice and Public Order Act 1994 *increased maximum sentence for children from 1 to 2 years*).

Custodial sentences for young offenders

There are numerous custodial sentencing options available to the Youth Courts and the Youth Justice Board. These are as follows.

Detention and Training Orders (DTOs) (ss 73–79, CDA 1998)

- Two-part sentence combining: a period in custody and a period spent under supervision in the community (for 12–14-year-olds; can be 10-years-old if offence is sufficiently serious)

- Provisions for early or late release
- Emphasis on sentence planning
- Main aim: time spent in custody must be constructive
- 'Throughcare' programme (post-release) must include effective supervision and support.

Murder and other serious offences

Historically, the Home Secretary has had the power to set a tariff to be served in cases where a young person has been sentenced to be detained during 'Her Majesty's Pleasure' (HMP) as a result of committing murder (or other serious offences such as rape) under the age of 18. However, in December 1999, the European Court of Human Rights (ECHR) in the case of Thompson and Venables (the two 10-year-old boys who killed James Bulger in 1993) found that HMP breached Convention rights. The *Criminal Justice and Court Services Act 2000* now gives the sentencing court the task of setting the tariff to be served (rather than the Home Secretary).

Detention During Her Majesty's Pleasure

This is the only sentence available to the courts for a person convicted of murder aged over 10 but under 18 at the time of the offence.

Detention (imprisonment) for Public Protection (IPP)

For juveniles this 'Public Protection Sentence' is classed as a sentence of *detention* rather than imprisonment. Where a juvenile has committed an offence carrying a maximum penalty of 10 years or more (manslaughter, rape, serious armed robbery etc), the court must consider whether an *Extended Sentence for Public Protection* would be an appropriate punishment before imposing a sentence of Detention for Public Protection. This new sentence came into effect on 4 April 2005 and applies to offences committed on or after that date.

Custody for Life

This is the mandatory sentence for a person aged 18 or over but under 21 at the time of the offence, who is convicted of murder and sentenced whilst under 21. It is also a discretionary sentence for those in this age group convicted of other offences for which a maximum sentence of life imprisonment can be passed on as an adult.

Young persons in prison and reconviction rates

- March 2004: 2565 children (aged 12–17) in prison (5% less than in 2003)
- March 2004: 11,019 young people in prison (aged 18–21)
- 42% are first-time offenders
- Reconviction rate within two years for young males (18–21s) is 71% (1999)
- Reconviction rate within two years for children (14–17s) is 80% (1999)
- More than two-thirds of boys are convicted for property crimes
- Average literacy age is 7-years-old
- Over 50% have been in care homes
- Over 45% have been excluded from school
- 85% have personality disorder (16–20-year-olds)
- Over 50% have drug dependency (16–20-year-olds)
- 25% of young offenders are fathers.

Sources: Youth Justice Board Statistics and
Office of National Statistics, ONS, 2000;
HM Chief Inspector of Prisons Annual Report, 2002–03.
See also Jennings (2003) *One Year Juvenile
Reconviction Rates: First Quarter of 2001 Cohort.*

Common pitfalls: You may have to answer the question 'Does prison work for young offenders?' – these are the areas you should address and watch out for:

- When writing about young persons in prison, you will do well to cite some of the reconviction rates for children leaving prison (see list above)
- Mention that reconviction rates for young males have remained consistently high (around 85% of all 14–16-year-olds within two years released from prison, 1999)
- 62% reoffended so seriously, they re-entered custody (1999)
- Black youngsters are over-represented in prison (15% of 15–17s are black compared with 2% of the general youth prison population).

"When a child is said to come from a 'dysfunctional' background, does this mean they have to become deviant?"

This question addresses criminological issues such as: criminogenic factors; why some young people become criminals and others don't; familial background and inequality and crime issues.

"What situational factors might help to explain youth crime?"

Here you need to look at the 'youth problem' in relation to anomie and strain theories; youth subcultures and the adolescent personality (so-called 'positivist' criminology).

"How would you explain gender-based differences in rates and frequency of offending?"

In this very difficult question you need to explore different rates of offending between girls and boys (men and women), also known as 'gender crime'. Anne Campbell (1981) argues, for instance, that when young women commit crime they follow the same pattern as young men in terms of which acts they commit; they just don't get caught as frequently as young men. Why do you think this is so?

"Has prison worked for young offenders? Discuss."

With a reoffending rate averaging about 78% for young offenders released from prison within two years, you need to look at the comparison of whether community punishment has had better results for young offenders than prison, as well as how youth custody deals (or not) with young offenders' rehabilitation.

"Discuss the ways and means in which a Youth Court can punish a young offender today."

You should look at legislation (e.g. *Crime and Disorder Act 1998*; *Youth Justice and Criminal Evidence Act 1999*; *Anti-Social Behaviour Act 2003*; *Criminal Justice Act 2003* etc) in order to answer this question; list the catalogue of punishment orders in the community that can be ordered by the (Youth) courts today, as well as the principal function of the Youth Justice Board and YOTs.

Taking it **FURTHER**

You may wish to study the topic of 'youth and crime' in more detail, particularly in relation to **criminalisation** or **gender** issues, as well as deviance in relation to family background and causes for young offending (e.g. **inequality**). Here are a few suggestions, such as government publications that relate to youthful reoffending or imprisonment:

1. **Home Office White Paper '*No More Excuses*: A New Approach to Tackling Youth Crime in England and Wales', 1997 by the then Home Secretary Jack Straw**
   The Home Office publication gives you the full range of measures available to youth justice and law enforcement agencies today by means of the *Crime and Disorder Act 1998*. The White Paper 1997 was based on 'The Review of Delay in the Criminal Justice System' by Martin Narey (The *Narey Report*, February 1997) introducing measures to speed up particularly the youth Criminal Justice System across England and Wales. Subsequent pilots – undertaken by the consultants Ernst and Young – in six youth justice areas showed that these measures halved the time taken to deal with young offenders in the criminal courts, and to cut the time from first charge to disposal from 89.5 days to 37.9 days. The initiatives were piloted in Tyneside, Croydon/Bromley/Sutton, North Staffordshire, North Wales, Blackburn and Burnley, and Northamptonshire between October 1998 and March 1999. The required legislation was introduced by the *Crime and Disorder Act 1998*. The measures introduced for adult and young offenders were 'early first hearings' for straightforward guilty pleas and 'early administrative hearings' for all other cases.

2. **Social Exclusion Unit (2002) *Reducing Re-Offending by Ex-Prisoners*. London: TSO**
   Reports by the Social Exclusion Unit are interesting, and deal with the inequality and crime phenomenon; they examine how society deals with the causes of crime, and point to the young offender as the victim of circumstances over which he has no control.

3. **What are children sent to prison for?**
   Study the table below and comment on why children are given prisons sentences. Compare violent and non-violent offences in your analysis.

Children sentenced to immediate custody during 1999

Offence	Boys	Girls
Violence against the person	15%	27%
Sexual offences	2%	–
Burglary	22%	6%
Robbery	13%	10%
Theft and handling	25%	27%
Fraud and forgery	less than 1%	1%
Drug offences	2%	4%
Other	20%	22%
Not recorded	2%	3%
Total Number	**5523**	**354**

Source: Prison Statistics, England and Wales, Home Office 1999.

Textbook guide

BROWN, S. AND MACMILLAN, J. (1998) *Understanding Youth and Crime: listening to youth?* Oxford: OUP.

CAMPBELL, A. (1981) *Girl Delinquents.* Oxford: Blackwell.

FITZGERALD, M., STOCKDALE, J. AND HALE, C. (2003) *Young People and Street Crime.* London: The Youth Justice Board.

MUNCIE, J. (2004) *Youth and Crime.* 2nd ed. London: Sage.

2.9	
prisons	

Whilst prison is serving its purpose as the ultimate form of punishment in most western European countries prison can also be an isolating and brutal experience for the offender. Research has found that first-time imprisonment can be particularly traumatic for vulnerable people i.e. those with mental health problems, drug addicts or the young.

This section introduces the reader firstly to the history of the prison, dating back to the early 18th century with key thinkers like Jeremy Bentham and the notion of the so-called 'Benthamite' ideal of the 'all seeing' Panopticon Penitentiary. You will be introduced to the basic principles of penological theory with some penal reform policies of the 20th and 21st centuries.

Secondly, you will read about prison overcrowding and reasons for this. The section ends with prison privatisation and explains why the penal establishment has become big business today. But famous penologists and prison reformers will have you believe that imprisonment should remain the 'last resort' for a sentencing judge, with custody as the harshest sanction available to English criminal courts.

Core areas: **History of imprisonment**

The prison system: organisation and structures

The use of custody

Rise in the prison population

Private prisons

National Offender Management Service (NOMS)

Does prison work?

Reconviction rates and suicides

Rehabilitation of offenders

Prisoners and human rights.

Learning outcomes

By the end of this section you should be able to:

- Demonstrate a basic knowledge of the history of imprisonment
- Illustrate and appreciate penal policies of the 20th and 21st centuries
- Give a detailed account of different types of prisons; and
- Critically analyse the use and purpose of imprisonment
- Portray the main issues relating to prison privatisation.

Running themes

- Punishment
- Inequality
- Victims and crime
- Human rights
- Gender
- Race.

History of imprisonment

Most sanctions for 'convicts' during the 16th and 17th centuries tended to be community events, designed to publicly shame the offender in order to deter others (deterrence theory). Some of these public events included the ducking stool, the pillory, whipping, branding and the stocks. Until the early 19th century, the penitentiary (prison) was very rarely used as **punishment** in its own right. Evidence suggests that local 'gaols' during this period were badly maintained and often controlled 'privately' by negligent 'gaolers'. Many people died of diseases like gaol fever, a form of typhus.

The first 'modern' Benthamite star-shaped prison in England was London's *Pentonville Prison* which is still in use today. Pentonville was built between 1842–44, using the panoptical design (see p. 115). It was originally designed to hold 520 prisoners (male and female), each held in a cell measuring 13 feet long, 7 feet wide and 9 feet high. The use of solitary confinement ('separate and silent system') for 'rule infractions' was rigidly enforced even in the prison chapel. Within six years of Pentonville, 54 new prisons were built using the panoptical template.

Key thinkers

- **John Howard** (1726–90) was a famous prison reformer (the 'Howard League for Penal Reform' is named after him). He was born in London, and was a wealthy property owner in Bedfordshire. A man of austere religious habits which he also proposed for the rehabilitation of prisoners. As Sheriff of Bedfordshire from 1773, he learnt that acquitted prisoners could only leave gaol once they had paid the gaoler's fee. This led Howard to embark upon an extraordinary life of prison visits throughout the British Isles and most of Europe. His epical works *The State of the Prisons in England and Wales* (1777) exposed the squalor and brutality in 16 English County Gaols, 38 prisons in the British Isles (including Royal Hospital, Plymouth; Bedford County Gaol; London's Newgate), and seven on the Continent (including Houses of Correction in Breda and Utrecht, Netherlands; la Maison de Force in Ghent, Belgium; House of Correction in Rome; the House of Correction in St. Petersburg, Russia; and the Hotel-Dieu in Lyons, France). Howard died of typhus on a visit to Russia and was buried there.
- **Jeremy Bentham** (1748–1832). In 1791, the Anglo-American Philosopher proposed an architectural innovation designed to lead to 'safe and humane' prisons. Bentham's 'Central Gaol' became known as the *Panopticon*.

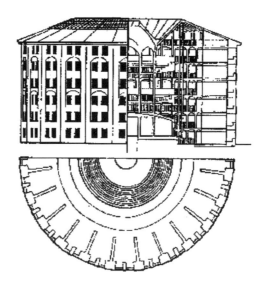

The Panopticon

This 'all-seeing place' (*pan-opticon*) was designed to provide complete observation of every prisoner. Bentham's *Panopticon* represented central control through isolation with the possibility of constant surveillance. Solid walls between the cells prevented any communication between prisoners, and a small window in the back of the cell would let in light to illuminate the contents. At the centre of the ring of cells, Bentham placed an observation tower with special shutters to prevent the prisoners from seeing the guards.

Pentonville Prison 1842

- **Gladstone, Sir William Ewart** (1809–98) British Tory Prime Minister (changed to Liberal) and statesman (1868–74, 1880–85, 1886, 1892–94). After the General Election of 1892, the then Home Secretary (Lord) Asquith ordered an inquiry into the state of prisons. The then Secretary of State, Gladstone, responsible for prisons, set up inquiry. Gladstone described prison conditions as the 'most shaming sanctions' and 'outdated'. The *Gladstone Report* (1895) brought about penal reform with an impact on prison conditions into the 20th century. Positive recommendations concentrated on pre-trial detention, cellular prison labour and solitary confinement, and the Borstal system for young offenders.
- **Michel Foucault** (1926–84 Poitiers, France). As a Social Scientist and Criminologist he carried out research into psychiatric practices in mental hospitals and published papers on psychopathy and mental illness. In *Discipline and Punish* (1975) Foucault observed that the notion of 'human control' no longer required physical domination over the body, but could be achieved through isolation and the constant possibility of observation (i.e. the prison). The prison, he argued, became the state's 'power of mind over mind' – used as a form of physical intimidation. Prison, he noted, embodies all modern control techniques for a state to punish its individuals. Foucault called this

'Panopticism' and stated that the major effect of the *Panopticon* was: 'to induce in the inmate a state of conscious and permanent visibility that assures the automatic functioning of power … that this architectural apparatus should be a machine for creating and sustaining a power relation independent of the person who exercises it; in short, that the inmates should be caught up in a power situation of which they are themselves the bearers … The Panopticon is a machine for dissociating the seeing–being seen dyad: in the peripheic ring, one is totally seen, without ever seeing; in the central tower, one sees everything without ever being seen.' (1975: pp. 195–228).

The prison system: organisation and structures

By 2005, there were 140 prison establishments in England and Wales, run by the government (Home Office) agency, *Her Majesty's Prison Service* (HMPS), presently known as the National Offender Management Service (NOMS), now comprising prison and probation services. The prison estate includes high security prisons (also known as Category A), local and remand prisons (Category B), Training prisons (Category C), Young Offender Institutions (YOIs) (for sentenced prisoners under the age of 21), open and semi-open prisons (Categories D and E) and some remand centres.

Prison population and accommodation

Population May 2005

Male	71,516
Female	4,501
Total	**76,017**

Certified Normal Accommodation (CNA)	77,287

Number under Home Detention Curfew Supervision (electronic tagging)	3,337

Population May 2004

Male	70,623
Female	4,610
Total	**75,233**

Certified Normal Accommodation (CNA)	75,731

Number under Home Detention Curfew supervision (electronic tagging)	3,588

Source: HM Prison Service, Population Figures at 27 May 2005.

The use of custody

The increase in the prison population over the past decade (since 1994) can largely be attributed to the *increase in sentence length* by justices, particularly for 'serious offences' (e.g. drug trafficking). But other offences were attracting longer sentences too: by 2004, first-time *domestic burglars* were twice as likely to receive a custodial sentence than, say, some eight years previously. At the same time, the number of short sentences had also increased. The HM Prison Service has the following aims and objectives:

- To protect the public by holding those committed by the courts in a safe, decent and healthy environment
- To reduce crime by providing constructive regimes which address offending behaviour, improve educational work abiding behaviour in custody and after release.

In order to substantiate your argument about the rise in the English prison population, you might find some of these facts and figures useful to back your argument.

Fact file on prisons in England/ Wales

- *Total prison population stood at 74,960 – March 2004 (an increase of 2484 over one year)*
- *Increase of 25,000 prisoners over ten years (1993–2003)*
- *May 1997 (Labour came to Government) prison population at 60,131*
- *1992 – average prison population at 46,000*
- *Imprisonment rate 141 (per 100,000 of the population – March 2004)*
- *Imprisonment rate 44% higher than Germany (98 per 100,000)*
- *Imprisonment rate 52% higher than France (93 per 100,000)*
- *Of 138 prisons nine are 'privatised' (contracted-out – March 2004)*
- *Since May 1997, seven new prisons opened with 14,700 additional places*
- *52% of all prisoners released (2003) reconvicted within two years.*

Female prisoners

The number of female prisoners has more than tripled over the past decade. In 1993 the female prison population stood at 1580. At 26 March

2004 there were 4589 women in prison representing about 6% of the total prisoner population in England and Wales. Women represent 51.3% of the overall population in England and Wales. There were 4461 females in custody on Friday 7 November 2004 – a slight drop. The female prison estate comprises of the following:

Askham Grange	Drake Hall	Morton Hall
Brockhill	East Sutton Park	New Hall
Bronzefield	Eastwood Park	Send
Buckley Hall	Edmunds Hill	Styal
Bullwood Hall	Foston Hall	Female wing at HMP
Cookham Wood	Holloway	Winchester (Durham's 'she'
Downview	Low Newton	wing was closed in 2004).

It is worth noting that fewer than 20% of women have committed crimes of violence; the Howard League and the Prison Reform Trust have long argued that most women are no danger to the public and should not serve a prison sentence at all, especially since many women have to run their families from inside prison (looking after children or elderly parents).

Life-sentence prisoners

The number of life-sentence prisoners ('lifers') has increased. By November 2003, there were 5475 prisoners serving life sentences. This compared with fewer than 4000 in 1998, and 3000 in 1992. This means that England has not only the highest imprisonment rate in industrialised western Europe, but also one of the highest lifer populations. On 28 February 2005, there were 5792 prisoners serving a life sentence (5606 men; 186 women; 186 young offenders). There are several types of life sentence:

- Mandatory Life Sentence
- Discretionary Life Sentence
- Automatic Life Sentence
- Imprisonment for Public Protection (IPP)
- Detention for Life
- Tariff
- Release on Life Licence
- Supervision and Recall.

Rise in the prison population

There has been a dramatic rise in the total prison population over the past ten years. Between 1992–2002, the number of adults sent to prison for sentences of less than 12 months, more than doubled from 18,500 to nearly 48,000. In 2002 more than half of all those sent to prison were there for prison terms of less than six months.

Fact file on imprisonment

✓ December 2003 there were 12,233 on remand (remands)
✓ Number of female prisoners has increased dramatically
✓ March 1994 female prison population stood at 1811
✓ March 2004 there were 4477 woman in prison
✓ 66% of female prisoners are mothers; and
✓ An estimated 17,700 children are separated from their mother by imprisonment
✓ March 2004 there were 11,019 young offenders in prisons (under 21)
✓ 2565 young prisoners were under 18.

Private prisons

Public–private partnerships have long been established in Britain in private prison management (so-called Private Finance Initiative – PFI). Since the inception of Britain's first private prison, *HMP Wolds* near Hull in 1992 (with the legal backing of the CJA 1991), it has been established that private sector involvement in the HM Prison Service and the Scottish Prison Service have helped to drive costs down and improve performance in the prisons run by the public sector.

Please make a note that Britain is now the country with the most privatised (contracted-out) prisons. All newly commissioned prison establishments are designed, built and managed (DBM) by the private sector, using considerable mixed management approaches under PFI.

Private sector prisons are subject to a series of controls in the same way as are prisons managed by the HM Prison Service. They are all subject to scrutiny by Parliament and to inspection by HM Chief Inspector of

Prisons. Furthermore, they are required by contract to comply with the Prison Rules, Prison Service Orders and Instructions.

By 2005, about 5% of the total English prison estate was privately run, holding around 5000 prisoners (i.e. about 7% of the total prison population). Of the 139 prisons in 2005, there were nine privately run prisons in England and Wales.

National Offender Management Service (NOMS)

Following extensive consultation in January 2004 by the Home Office, with some 400 different agencies and responses involved, the then Home Secretary David Blunkett, decided to create the concept and practice of 'end-to-end offender management'. There would be greater competition within 'Correctional Services' meaning greater contracting-out (privatisation) of the prison estate. The 42 regional Probation Boards have remained, allowing for local links with other Criminal Justice agencies. Regional Offender Managers (ROMs) were appointed to manage ten NOMS – regions, taking direct responsibility for budget allocation and 'contracting-in' services.

What are the responsibilities of NOMS?

Achieving reduction in reoffending by adequate punishment and rehabilitation of offenders, that will lead to ...

- *Ensuring a safer society for all*
- *Ensuring that custodial punishments make offenders address their criminal behaviour*
- *Offering realistic possibilities for a 'crime-free' life after prison (e.g. through education and work inside prisons)*
- *Raising educational standards among offenders in order to break the link between low educational attainment and criminality*
- *Forging and supporting effective links with complementary services in offender rehabilitation (police, health services, education, employment)*
- *Increasing contracting-out (privatisation) provision of prisons and related services.*

Does prison work?

In the course of your studies, you may well be asked: 'What is prison for?' and 'Does prison work?' The answers you can give are manifold; you should present all sides of a learned argument advanced in the literature.

> **Common pitfalls:** When writing an essay on the 'Does prison work?' subject, you are advised not to base your entire opinion on popular culture or the press, but use learned sources (*primary* sources, e.g. HM Prison Service and Home Office figures, and *secondary* sources in the form of literature sources).

Reconviction rates and suicides

As early as 1988, reconviction rates for adult males, released from prison within two years, stood at 55% and at 75% for teenagers. If prison is used inappropriately it can cause more crime and *reconviction* rates prove this. By 2003, the reconviction rate for young male offenders released from prison had not changed and remained at 75%; similarly for adult males at 52%. The reconviction rate for females had been 57% and now stood at 45% respectively.

Reconviction rates

- 52% of all prisoners released are reconvicted within two years
- Younger people are more likely to be reconvicted (about 78%).

Prison suicides

First-timers in prison and young offenders can find the effects of being imprisoned very stressful indeed. Ultimately, this can lead to self-harm and suicide incidents, which are very high in prisons. In 2002, there were 94 deaths in custody, a rise of 29% compared with the previous year. This included 14 women (compared with nine in 2001). In 2003, there were 105 recorded suicides in prisons, a 40% increase compared with the previous years.

Rehabilitation of offenders

In terms of rehabilitation within the prison sense, the starting point of your thinking should be that the likelihood of (re)offending should be reduced, given that prisoners might undergo education, vocational training and work programmes whilst serving their sentence, as part of their 'sentence plan'. During the mid-1990s, several positive moves were made in this direction by the Prison Service; one such programme was that of 'Prison Industries' comprising of rehabilitative work programmes involving prisoners in real industrial work inside the prison 'factory'.

The *Prisoners Earnings Act 1996* was passed, providing for prisoners to earn wages at a level enabling them to support dependants, pay victim compensation, and save significant amounts for their release date. By the late 1990s, there was real Prison Service investment in setting up work-based training and accreditation programmes (i.e. National Vocational Qualifications – NVQs).

What constitutes rehabilitation in prison?

- *Prison industries and prisoner labour*
- *Vocational, educational and skills training programmes*
- *Cognitive-behavioural programmes*
- *Therapeutic Communities (Grendon and Dovegate Prisons)*
- *Throughcare (e.g. post-release prisoner employment, accommodation, family links and support etc).*

Prisoners and human rights

There have been a large number of **human rights** legal challenges (before the English and the Strasbourg Human Rights Court) objecting to the treatment of prisoners whilst in custody contra the *Prison Rules 1999* (The *Prison Rules 1964* were re-written after the *Human Rights Act 1998*).

Now with the *Human Rights Act 1998* fully in place, the following are the main ECHR-articles which influence and impact on prisons and the prisoner:

- Article 2: right to life
- Article 3: prohibits the use of torture and the infliction of degrading or inhumane treatment and/or punishment
- Articles 5 and 6: aimed primarily at the conduct of criminal proceedings
- Article 7: places strict limitations on retrospective criminal laws
- Articles 9 and 10: focus on the freedom of thought, conscience, religious belief and expressions.

Prisoners continue being ill-treated and racially abused within prisons. In September 2001, three prison officers were convicted of ill-treating prisoners in *Wormwood Scrubs Prison*, during the 1990s. The Director of the Prison Service, Martin Narey raised the issue of prison overcrowding and inhumane and 'immoral' treatment in the English prisons during the Prison Governor's Association (PGA) annual conference in February 2001. Narey threatened to resign unless prison governors fully supported his plans to improve failing jails. Commissioner of the National Offender Management Service (NOMS), Martin Narey, then announced in July 2005, that he was leaving NOMS to become Chief Executive of Barnardo's children's charity, due to his 'disenchantment with NOMS' (Source: BBC News Online, 1 July 2005).

" How far can the emergence of the penitentiary of the mid 19th century be considered a success or failure? Discuss. "

Here you need to look at the history of the prison, and give reasons why the prison continues to be so 'popular'. Use some of the learned literature e.g. Foucault.

" What is the purpose of imprisonment? "

You need to look at the Prison Service's aims and objectives (e.g. punish, protect the public from future harm, rehabilitate the offender etc).

" How would you explain the growth of imprisonment? "

Look at changes in sentencing, and the increase in (longer) sentences; for example, look at life sentences, or female and youth imprisonment.

" Does prison work? "

This requires a similar answer and approach as Question 1.

" What is meant by prison privatisation? Discuss. "

You need to read around this subject; there is plenty of literature. Don't forget the political and penal policy aspect here, e.g. Thatcher/Conservative Government; *Criminal Justice Act 1991* etc.

Taking it **FURTHER**

Study the following statements by influential civil servants and prison managers. Comment on the rising prison population and high levels of overcrowding. What might be the possible negative effects resulting from these conditions?

Commentary 1

The conditions in which prisoners have to live in overcrowded cells, cells in which they have to eat together and in which they have to defecate in front for one another are, we know, deeply inadequate … but where we unnecessarily allow prisoners to languish in doubled up cells nearly all day and every day, the inadequate becomes the unacceptable. (Martin Narey, Commissioner for Correctional Services, Prison Service Conference, February 2003)

Commentary 2

It's important we don't overuse [prison]. It's expensive, it is disruptive to the loved ones of those who come inside, often entirely innocent families and children whose whole life has to change as a result, it's a difficult experience to get through. It shouldn't be used lightly. (Phil Wheatley, Director General of the HM Prison Service, speaking on *Breakfast with Frost*, 17 August 2003)

Commentary 3

As the prison population continues to rise, the fundamentals of prison life and regimes are under threat in many prisons: the ability even to provide a safe and decent environment for a growing, and increasingly damaged and demanding population. (Ann Owers, Chief Inspector of Prisons, Annual Report 2002/3, January 2004)

Textbook guide

CAVADINO, M. AND DIGNAN, J. (2001) *The Penal System. 2nd ed. London: Sage.*

MORRIS, N. AND ROTHMAN, D.J. (eds) (1995) *The Oxford History of the Prison. Oxford: OUP.*

MUNCIE, J. (2001) *'Prisons, Punishment and Penalty' in McLaughlin, E. and Muncie, J. (eds) (2001) Controlling Crime. 2nd ed. London: Sage.*

SMARTT, U. (2001) *Grendon Tales: stories from a therapeutic community. Winchester: Waterside Press.*

2.10	
probation	

You will by now have realised that the Criminal Justice System is a complex issue. The final agency now needed to complete your jigsaw of the Criminal Justice System is the National Probation Service (NPS), a major component in reducing crime. As a new national forum, the NPS now forms part of the National Offender Management Service (NOMS) to meet sentencers' needs.

This section addresses the changing role of the Probation Officer, who is no longer simply faced with offering support to released offenders. The work of a Probation Officer now comprises a vast catalogue of tasks, such as the supervision of the generic Community Sentence (Community Punishment Orders), formulating Pre-Sentence Reports (PSR) to the requirement of bringing prosecutions before the courts of those who have breached bail conditions, of fine defaulters and those offenders who disobey the Community Sentence – such breaches are punishable by imprisonment only.

Core areas: **The work of the National Probation Service: past and present**
Court work and sentencing
Community Sentence
Work in prisons
Probation Service and NOMS.

Learning outcomes

By the end of this section you should be able to:

- Illustrate the main role and function of the National Probation Service (NPS)
- Describe a Pre-Sentence Report (PSR) and give detailed criteria for a PSR
- Take into account the multi-disciplinary approach to a Community Sentence
- Appreciate the multi-disciplinary approach of community punishment
- Identify the complexities of the National Offender Management Service (NOMS) in relation to prisons and probation.

Running themes

- Human rights
- Victims of crime
- Punishment
- Criminalisation
- Crime and the media
- Fear of crime.

The work of the National Probation Service: past and present

When we hear about the work of Probation, the word 'Decarceration' often springs to mind. *Decarceration* is a deliberate move away from sending people to prison. *Decarcerationists* believe that prison walls should be torn down and that a criminal's punishment should be in the community (alternative sanctions). Decarceration has been associated with the *Abolitionist Movement* in Scandinavia and North America by Social Scientists and Criminologists such as Stanley Cohen.

Decarceration comprises:

- Community punishment orders (Community Sentence)
- Non-custodial punishment
- Community care (rehabilitation of offenders in the community)
- Drug treatment orders
- Home Detention Curfew (electronic tagging).

You should be aware of the fact that the Probation Service has undergone substantial changes since 2000. On 1 April 2001, the *National Probation Service of England and Wales* (NPS) was launched (*Criminal Justice and Court Services Act 2000*) replacing the old system of 54 separate regional probation services. Now the NPS is divided into 42 operational areas and Regional Boards under the auspices of the Home Office; these areas are coterminous with police borders and CPS administrative regions.

Today's role of a Probation Officer is no longer presented as offering support and assistance to offenders, but rather to assess and mange the risk the offender may pose to the public. Probation now oversees a large programme of community sentences ordered by the courts. Breaches of such orders have to be strictly enforced and are punishable only by imprisonment.

The Home Office identifies the key aims of the NPS as being to:

- *Protect the public*
- *Reduce reoffending*
- *Provide for the proper punishment of offenders*
- *Ensure offenders are aware of the effects of their crimes on their victims and on the public*
- *Rehabilitate offenders.*

Key thinkers

- **Stanley Cohen** (1922–) Born in Brooklyn, he grew up in South Africa and came to London in 1963 to work as a Social Worker. He was appointed Visiting Professor to the London School of Economics in 1994. As one of the most famous Criminologists, Cohen developed the concept of the 'moral panic' – an occurrence which is characterised by 'stylised and stereotypical' representation by the **mass media**, and a tendency for those 'in power' (politicians, bishops, editors etc) to man the 'moral barricades' and pronounce judgement. Cohen pointed out that the **media** report bad behaviour (he gave the classic example of 'Mods and Rockers' in the 1960s) in an exaggerated and distorted way thus increasing the **fear of crime**. Mods and Rockers became 'folk devils' of their time (see Cohen's *Folk Devils and Moral Panics: The Creation of the Mods and Rockers*, 1972).
- **John Braithwaite** (1951–) born in Ipswich, Australia, Professor of Law and Criminology at Australia National University, has undertaken extensive criminological research into *reintegrative shaming*. His concept of *shaming* rests on the stigmatisation of the deviant/criminal or criminal groups, which then turns them into 'outcasts'. According to Braithwaite, reintegrative shaming is a form of (society's) disapproval dispensed within an original relationship with the offender based on respect. The 'shaming' element focuses on the evil or the deed (offence) rather than on the offender. In turn, the offender is made to apologise (to the victim or members of society). In his *Crime, Shame and Reintegration* (1989) Braithwaite's theory is concerned with repentance for and reparation for the harm done through crime to society, and he is a strong protagonist in defence of *community punishment* and *restorative justice*, rather than prison (*Decarcerationist*). Braithwaite highlights the notion of *Communitarianism* (punishment in the community and alternative sanctions) which makes *shaming* possible and aids the rehabilitation of the offender. Braithwaite's argument against punitive justice systems and for *restorative justice* (RJ) established that there are good theoretical and empirical grounds for anticipating that well-designed RJ processes will restore victims, offenders, and communities better than existing Criminal Justice practices (e.g. prison).

Court work and sentencing

In 2002, the National Probation Service (NPS) introduced a commonly structured offender risk assessment programme known as OASys (Offender Assessment System) which assists the court in the sentencing decision making process. OASys is now used by all courts:

- Offenders on whom the courts have requested a Pre-sentence Report (PSR);
- All adult offenders on community penalties (Community Sentence orders);
- Hostel Residents on bail;
- Those released from prison on licence.

NPS records identified 244, 582 offenders as having received one or more electronic OASys assessments completed by probation staff between October 2002 and mid-January 2005. In addition there were several thousand assessments completed on the paper-based OASys system which the IT e-OASys progressively replaced, but these are not counted. The principle aim of the new offender assessment system is to ensure that particularly high-risk offenders are comprehensively assessed before they are released into the community (e.g. sexual or violent offences).

The writing of a PSR in court now involves sentencers (e.g. Magistrates) indicating to the Probation Service specific views on the offender's seriousness and perceived (future) risk to the public. This is done post-conviction, when justices consider either custody or the (generic) Community Sentence as a form of punishment. It is, of course, a matter for the court to decide if they would like to request a PSR, and if they do, the Probation Service is under statutory duty to provide one.

The court gives an initial indication of seriousness when requesting a report but may review its view of seriousness as a result of information presented to it. A Probation report may uncover aggravating features of the offence not previously known to the court.

Probation also runs Probation and Bail Hostels. In 2001, there were 100 Probation Hostels, providing 2060 beds for people awaiting trial, or for people on a community sentence, or following release from prison.

What is the sentencing purpose defined in the CJA 2003?

- *Punishment of offenders*
- *Reduction of crime (including by deterrence)*
- *Reform and rehabilitation of offenders*
- *Protection of the public*
- *Reparation.*

Pre-Sentence Reports (PSR) inform the court about:

- Suggested Sentence (e.g. Community Sentence; Conditional Discharge)
- Number, frequency and length of sessions for programme requirements
- Work to be undertaken and frequency of contact for supervision requirements
- What the offender will have to do and on how many occasions attendance will be required for activity requirements
- Details of what is prohibited in prohibited activity requirements.

Community Sentence

In April 2005, a generic *Community Sentence* was introduced under the CJA 2003. This provides nationally enhanced forms of 'community punishment orders' supervised by Probation. In 1999, 50,417 offenders began what was formerly known as a 'Community Service Order' (*Criminal Justice and Court Services Act 2000*), benefiting thousands of people with millions of hours of unpaid labour (e.g. street cleaning; graffiti removal; assistance in care homes). A *Community Sentence* is divided into three (punishment) bands with discounts for guilty pleas.

The Sentencing Guidelines Council (SGC) provides standard definitions for report writing (PSRs), linked to the seriousness of the offence.

	Short	Medium	Long
Unpaid work	40–80 hours	80–150 hours	150–300 hours
Supervision	Up to 12 months	12–18 months	12–36 months
Curfew	Up to 2 months	2–3 months	4–6 months

All existing community sentences and punishment orders now have an equivalent in the new sentencing structure under the CJA 2003, as set out in the table below.

The NPS has a statutory responsibility towards **victims of crime**. Restorative justice (RJ) was established under the *Crime and Disorder Act 1998*, and has been successfully practised in the youth justice reforms (CDA 1998 plus *Youth Crime and Criminal Evidence Act 1999*). Probation now also involved in adult RJ programmes, expanded under the CJA 2003 (in addition to the CDA 1998).

The NPS has a duty to ask victims or their families if they want to be consulted about the release arrangements for violent or sexual offenders sentenced to over 12 months. Victims will be kept informed of release arrangements and licence conditions, and should be offered support by Probation Officers. When release on licence is being considered victims views should be passed on to the appropriate body, e.g. as the Parole Board.

Criminal Justice Act 2003 – Community Order Requirements

Level of Seriousness	Requirement	Length	Main Purpose(s)
Low Medium High	**Unpaid work**	40–80 hours 80–150 hours 150–300 hours	Punishment Reparation Rehabilitation
Low Medium High	**Supervision**	Up to 12 months 12–18 months 12–36 months	Rehabilitation
Medium High	**Programme (Accredited)**	Stated number (or range) of sessions	Rehabilitation
Low Medium High	**Drug rehabilitation** Offender must consent	6 months 6–12 months 12–36 months	Rehabilitation
Low Medium High	**Alcohol treatment** Offender must consent	6 months 6–12 months 12–36 months	Rehabilitation
Medium High	**Mental health treatment** Offender must consent	Up to 36 months	Rehabilitation
Medium High	**Residence**	Up to 36 months	Rehabilitation
Medium High	**(Specified) Activity**	20–30 days Up to 60 days	Rehabilitation Reparation
Low Medium High	**Prohibited activity**	Up to 36 months	Punishment Protection
Low Medium High	**Exclusion**	Up to 2 months About 6 months About 12 months	Punishment Protection
Low Medium High	**Curfew** Typically up to 12 hours	Up to 2 months 2–3 months 4–6 months	Punishment Protection
Low	**Attendance Centre**	6–36 hours	Punishment

Old Order (until April 2005)	New Community Order Requirements (from April 2005)
Community Punishment Order (CPO)	Unpaid Work
Community Punishment and Rehabilitation Order (CPRO)	Unpaid Work Supervision (Programme)
Community Rehabilitation Order (CRO)	Supervision
CRO and Think First, Drink Impaired Drivers etc.	Supervision Programme (other requirements)
Intensive Change and Control Programme (ICCP)	Supervision Programme Activity (other requirements)
Drug Treatment and Testing Order (DTTO)	Drug Rehabilitation requirement Supervision (Accredited programme)

Restorative justice (RJ) and the adult justice system

- *Police cautioning; community policing and anti-social behaviour (e.g. acceptable behaviour contracts along ASBOs)*
- *PSRs can include RJ – may result in deferred sentence; conditional discharge (CD)*
- *Post sentence at request of victim or offender (part of victim support)*
- *Conditional cautions (last 6–9 months)*
- *Community Sentence can include RJ as an 'activity' requirement (e.g. domestic violence).*

All prisoners sentenced to more than 12 months are supervised on release, offenders given sentences of four years or more are released under more stringent conditions subject to assessment by the Parole Board (in December 2003, some 74,084 people were in prison, of whom 14% were serving a sentence of less than 12 months). For prisoners serving life sentences, contact with the Probation Service will continue indefinitely after release, and some sex offenders may also be given extended periods of post-release licence. It is the NPS's duty, jointly held with the police, to assess and manage the risk posed by all dangerous offenders released into the community.

Probation Service and NOMS

The Home Office launched the *National Offender Management Service* (NOMS) in January 2004. It was the intention that by June 2004, the Prison and Probation services would merge under NOMS into one 'Correctional Service' of England and Wales. There was to be a cluster of 'end-to-end' offender management regions (10 in total) of community prisons into 13 prison areas and 42 probation boards as one coherent organisation.

On 20 July 2004, the Home Secretary David Blunkett announced via Martin Narey (former Commissioner for Corrections) that the fusion of prisons and probation would not now take place. The result was that the 42 Regional Probation Boards were left in place with 42 Probation Chiefs. By November 2004, ten Regional Offender Managers (ROMs) were appointed, with governance over Community Prisons, 42 Probation Areas and public, voluntary or private services to assist the 'throughcare' of offenders. Christine Knott was appointed the National Offender Manager (of NOMS) – formerly Chief Probation Officer for Greater Manchester. One of the main functions of the ROMs is to commission additional services (e.g. drug treatment; sex offender treatment in the community; electronic tagging; supervision of probation orders etc). The Minister for Prisons and Probation, Paul Goggins, did not rule out private contractors and welcomed the assistance of voluntary agencies (e.g. Victim Support) in May 2005.

What are the responsibilities and functions of 42 Probation Boards within NOMS?

- *Responsible enforcement of Community Sentence and punishment orders*
- *Risk assessment of sentenced offenders (low, medium, high); and*
- *Encouraging Community Sentence for less serious offences*
- *Contracting-out additional services to assist rehabilitation of offenders*
- *Ensuring that community punishments make offenders address their behaviour*
- *Offering a crime-free path*
- *Law enforcement for breach of Community Sentence (via the courts).*

How NOMS will take shape in the near future is for you to find out and research further (see **Taking it further** section below). It is too soon to tell whether the new NOMS Agency – incorporating prisons and probation – is going to be successful in tackling persistent offending. Will it reduce the high recidivism and reconviction rate of around 57% for adult offenders, or the 78% young offender recidivism rate that still prevails today? It is for you to speculate and research further, particularly in the area of 'contracting-in' services via the private sector.

❝What is community punishment? How has the Probation Service's role changed since 2001? Discuss with reference to recent changes in legislation.❞

You need to look at the *Crime and Disorder Act 1998* and the *Criminal Justice Act 2003*, and discuss all the various changes in sentencing and the role Probation now plays (e.g. PSRs etc).

❝Would you say that the creation of NOMS has improved the management of offenders? Discuss with reference to the Probation Service's involvement in prisons and community punishment orders.❞

You need to be well informed regarding penal policy and the fast changing policies of ministers and Home Office policies. Undertake some extensive online research for this by using Home Office, Prison and Probation websites. Please note that the Commissioner of Corrections and NOMS resigned from his post in July 2005.

Taking it **FURTHER**

- Find out, how certain sectors of the prison and probation services under NOMS are contracted-out (i.e. privatised)
- How does the Probation Service deal with end-to-end offender management and their practical 'throughcare'?
- What happens to a released prisoner in terms of housing, work placement, education and family support?

Textbook guide

BROWNLEE, I. (1998) *Community Punishment: A Critical Introduction. London: Longman.*

MCLAUGHLIN, E., FERGUSSON, R., HUGHES, G. AND WESTMARLAND, L. (eds) (2003) *Restorative Justice: Critical Issues. London: Sage/The Open University.*

SULLIVAN, D. AND TIFFT, L. (2006) *Handbook of Restorative Justice: a global perspective: London: Routledge.*

WHITFIELD, D. (2001) *An Introduction to the Probation Service. 2nd ed. Winchester. Waterside Press.*

WORRALL, A. AND HOY, C. (eds) (2005) *Punishment in the Community: making offenders, making choices. Cullompton: Willan.*

part three*

study, writing and revision skills

General introduction

If you work your way carefully through this section, you should, at the end, be better equipped to profit from your lectures, benefit from your seminars, construct your essays efficiently, develop effective revision strategies and respond comprehensively to the pressures of exam situations. In the six sections that lie ahead, you will be presented with: checklists and bullet points to focus your attention on key issues; exercises to help you participate actively in the learning experience; illustrations and analogies to enable you to anchor learning principles in everyday events and experiences; and worked examples to demonstrate the use of such features as structure, headings and continuity. You should by now be used to the **Tips!** features which continue to provide practical advice in your course companion.

In the exercises that are presented here, students should decide how much effort they would like to invest in each exercise. It just depends on your individual preferences and requirements. You might prefer to read each section right through before going back to tackle some of the exercises. Suggested answers are provided after some of the exercises. The aim is to prompt you to reflect on your study material, remember what you have read and trigger your own thoughts. Space is provided for you to write your responses down in a few words; you may prefer to reflect on them within your own mind. However, writing will help you slow down and digest the material; what you write down is also grounded more

*in collaboration with David McIlroy

firmly in your mind and assists the process of memorising some of the more legalistic information (e.g. Acts of Parliament or cases).

Finally the overall aim of Part 3 is to point you to the notion of academic and personal development. By giving attention to these factors you will give yourself the toolkit you will need to excel and advance in your studies.

3.1

how to get the most out of your lectures

Learning outcomes

By the end of this section you should be able to:

- Make the most of your lecture notes

- Prepare your mind for new terms/vocabulary

- Develop an independent approach to learning

- Write efficient summary notes from lectures

- Take the initiative and build on your lectures.

Keeping in context

According to higher educational commentators and advisors, best quality learning is facilitated when it is set within an overall learning context (these are the **Learning outcomes** we have mentioned in each section of Part 2). It should be the responsibility of your lecturers or seminar tutors to provide a context for you to learn in by giving you the learning outcomes at the start of each lecture or at least in the course book provided. However, it is *your* responsibility to see to this overall context. You can do this even before your first lecture begins. Such a panoramic view can be achieved by becoming familiar with the outline content of both a given subject and the entire study programme (Part 2 has provided you with the 'Core Curriculum' in Criminal Justice).

Before you go into each lecture you should briefly remind yourself of where the **Running themes** fit into the overall scheme of things. Think, for example, of how more confident you will feel when you go to a new lecture and you have already heard some of the terms which your lecturer will be mentioning.

> *At the start of your Criminal Justice or Criminology course, you need to find your syllabus, get hold of the programmed reading list (set texts) and locate the position of each lecture and seminar/tutorial workshop. You may even have to undertake a work-placement, or work-shadowing programme (e.g. with the Crown Court Witness Service). In which case it is worthwhile sorting this out before the course starts.*

Use of lecture notes

It is always beneficial to do some preliminary reading before you enter a lecture. This course companion should help you get a 'handle' on what the study of Criminal Justice is all about. If lecture notes are provided in advance (e.g. electronically), then print these out, read over them and take them with you to the lecture. You can insert question marks or highlight issues where you will need further clarification. Some lecturers prefer to provide full notes, some prefer to make skeleton outlines available (e.g. on an overhead projector or via PowerPoint); some issue no notes at all!

If notes or handouts are provided, take full advantage of these and supplement them with your own notes from your set texts or the suggested additional reading from your course companion. Some basic preparation will equip you with a great advantage – you will be able to 'tune in' and think more clearly about the lecture than you would have done without the preliminary work.

> *Don't set yourself too many tedious tasks at the early stages of your academic programme. You may lose some motivation and momentum. Set yourself some short, simple achievement tasks that will 'lubricate' your mind. For example, you are more likely to start some preliminary reading in a general textbook (e.g. Elliott and Quinn's English Legal System) to prepare for a general introduction on the Criminal Justice System of England and Wales.*

Mastering 'foreign' terms

Let us assume that in an early lecture you are introduced to a series of new and 'foreign' terms such as: 'familial', 'empirical' or 'criminogenic'. Most likely, you will be hearing these terms for the first time. They may give you a headache! New words can be threatening, especially if you have to face a string of them in one lecture. Your course companion has provided you with a **Glossary** at the end of the book – make use of this, and Criminal Justice and Legal terms will be explained to help you.

Your confidence will greatly increase when you begin to follow the flow of arguments that contain technical or 'foreign' terms, and more especially when you can freely use these terms yourself in speaking and writing.

When you have heard a term a number of times it will not seem as daunting as it was initially. Some people may have a good recognition of vocabulary and they immediately know what a word means when they read it or hear it in context. Others have a good command of language when they speak; they have an ability to recall words freely. Still others are more fluent in recall when they write, and words seem to flow rapidly for them when they engage in the dynamics of writing. You can work at developing all three approaches in your course. The **Checklist** ✓ features may be of some help in mastering the terms you hear in lectures. In your case, it is certainly worth investing in the *Sage Dictionary of Criminology* (edited by Eugene McLaughlin and John Muncie, 2003).

Checklist: Mastering terms used in your lectures

✓ Read lecture notes before the lectures and list any unfamiliar terms
✓ Read over the listed terms until you are familiar with their sound
✓ Try to work out meanings of terms from their context
✓ Do not suspend learning the meaning of a term indefinitely
✓ Write out a sentence that includes the new word (do this for each word)
✓ Meet with other students and test each other with the technical terms
✓ Jot down new words you hear in lectures and check out the meaning soon afterwards.

Developing independent study

In the current educational ethos there are the twin aims of cultivating teamwork/group activities and independent learning. There is not necessarily a conflict between the two, as they should complement each other. For example, if you are committed to independent learning you have more to offer other students when you work in small groups, and you will also be prompted to follow up on the leads given by them. Furthermore, the guidelines given to you in lectures are designed to lead you into deeper independent study. The issues raised in lectures are pointers to provide direction and structure for your extended personal pursuit. Your aim should invariably be to build on what you are given, and you should never think of merely returning the bare bones of the lecture material in a course work essay or exam.

*It is always very refreshing to an examiner to be given work from a student that contains recent studies and new research that the examiner or reader of your piece of work may not have previously encountered. Keep up to date with particularly journals and periodicals (see **Key thinkers** and **Taking it further** sections). Locate these in your college or university library.*

Note-taking strategy

Note-taking in lectures is an art that you will only perfect with practice and by trial and error. At first, you may not be able to write speedily, especially if you are used to typing or word-processing your letters or pieces of work in the past. Each student should find the formula that works best for him or her. What works for one, does not work for the other. Some students can write more quickly than others, some are better at 'short hand' than others, and some are better at deciphering their own scrawl! The problem will always be to try to find a balance between concentrating beneficially on what you hear, and making sufficient notes that will enable you to later comprehend what you have heard. You should not, however, become frustrated by the fact that you will not understand or remember immediately everything you have heard.

Be present at lectures! This will give you a substantial advantage over those students who do not attend. Do not be tempted to tape-record a lecture (unless you have special needs). If you do, you should still take your own notes, and only use the tape recording to supplement your own notes. Only borrow notes from your fellow students if you really could not attend the lecture. Everyone's note-taking is individual, and you will most likely not understand someone else's hieroglyphs anyway.

Checklist: Note-taking in lectures

✓ Develop the note-taking strategy that works best for you
✓ Work at finding a balance between listening and writing
✓ Make some use of optimal short hand (e.g. a few key words may summarise a story)
✓ Use different colours (highlighter) to stress important words
✓ Underline each legal case with a ruler (or highlight)
✓ Too much writing may impair the flow of the lecture for you
✓ Some limited notes are better than none
✓ Good note-taking may facilitate deeper processing of information
✓ It is essential to 'tidy up' notes as soon as possible after a lecture
✓ Reading over notes soon after lectures will consolidate your learning.

Checklist: What to do during a lecture?

✓ If the lecturer invites questions, make a note of all the questions asked
✓ Try to interact with the lecture material by asking questions (best done at the end of the lecture)
✓ Highlight/underline points that you would like to develop in personal study
✓ Trace connections between the lecture and relevant parts of your core curriculum
✓ Bring together notes from the lecture and other sources (e.g. textbooks and source references in journal articles)
✓ Restructure the lecture outline into your own preferred format (e.g. use of bullet points)
✓ Think of ways in which aspects of the lecture material can be applied and illustrated (use examples)
✓ Follow up on issues of interest that have arisen out of the lecture (e.g. use the **Taking it further** and **Textbook guide** features).

3.2	
how to make the most of your seminars or tutorial workshops	

Learning outcomes

By the end of this section you should be able to:

- Be aware of the value of seminars
- Focus on links to learning
- Recognise qualities you can use repeatedly
- Manage potential problems in seminars/tutorials
- Prepare yourself adequately for seminars/tutorials.

Don't under-estimate seminars or tutorial workshops!

Seminars or tutorials (sometimes referred to as 'workshops') are often optional in a degree programme and sometimes poorly attended because they are underestimated. Some students may be convinced that the lecture is the truly authoritative way to receive quality information. Undoubtedly, lectures play an important role in an academic programme, but seminars have a unique contribution to learning that will complement lectures. Other students may feel that their time would be better spent in personal study. Again, private study is unquestionably essential for personal learning and development, but you will nevertheless diminish your learning experience if you neglect seminars. If seminars/tutorials were to be removed from academic programmes something really important would be lost: your personal contact with the course tutor, where you can ask questions. You should always prepare tutorial questions which have been set in advance.

Checklist: Advantages of seminars and tutorials

- ✓ Usually smaller groups than lectures
- ✓ Can identify problems that you had not thought of

✓ Can clear up confusing issues

✓ Allows you to ask questions and make comments

✓ Can help you develop friendships and teamwork

✓ Enables you to refresh and consolidate your knowledge

✓ Can help you sharpen motivation and redirect study efforts.

An asset to complement learning activities and learning outcomes

In higher education there is usually emphasis on variety in delivery, such as: learning experience, learning styles and assessment methods. The seminar or tutorial workshop is deemed to hold an important place within the overall scheme of teaching, learning and assessment. In your Criminal Justice or Criminology programmes, the seminars/tutorials are usually directly linked to the assessment tasks ahead of you, as well as the exam at the end of the course.

A key question that you should bring to every seminar or tutorial is 'How does this seminar/tutorial connect with my other learning activities and my assessments or exams?'

In a seminar/tutorial you will hear a variety of contributions, and different perspectives and emphases from your study colleagues. You will have the chance to interrupt and the experience of being interrupted! You will also learn that you can get things wrong and still survive! It is often the case that when one student admits that they did not know some important piece of information, other students quickly follow on to the same admission in the wake of this. If you can learn to ask questions and not feel stupid, then seminars will give you an asset for learning and a life-long educational quality.

Appoint someone to guide and control the discussion on a particular topic (e.g. Prison Privatisation). Invite individuals to prepare, in advance, to make a contribution. Hand out agreed discussion questions at some point prior to the seminar. Stress at the beginning that no-one should monopolise the discussion and emphasise that there must be no personal attacks on any individual (state clearly what this means). You could also invite and encourage quieter students to participate and assure each person that their contribution is valued.

An opportunity to contribute

If you have never made a contribution to a seminar or tutorial before, you may need something to use as an 'ice breaker'. It does not matter if your first contribution is only a sentence or two – the important thing is to make a start. One way to do this is to make brief notes as others contribute, and whilst doing this, a question or two might arise in your mind. If your first contribution is a question, that is a good start. Write it down! Or it may be that you will be able to point out some connection between what others have said, or identify conflicting opinions that need to be resolved. If you have already begun making contributions, it is important that you keep the momentum going, and do not allow yourself to lapse back into the safe cocoon of shyness.

Strategies for benefiting from your seminar experience

If you are required to bring a presentation to your seminar, you might want to consult a more complete textbook on presentation skills (such as the complementary study guide by McIllroy, 2003). Alternatively, you may be content with the summary checklists presented at the end of each section in Part 3 of this course companion.

Checklist: How to benefit from seminars

- ✓ Do some preparatory reading
- ✓ Familiarise yourself with the main ideas to be addressed
- ✓ Make notes during the seminar
- ✓ Make some verbal contribution – ask a question!
- ✓ Remind yourself of the skills you can develop
- ✓ Look at the Learning Skills
- ✓ Make brief bullet points on what you should follow up
- ✓ Read over your notes as soon as possible after the seminar
- ✓ Continue discussion with fellow students after the seminar has ended.

Checklist: How to give a presentation

- ✓ Be selective in what you choose to present
- ✓ Space out points clearly on visuals (large and legible – use at least Arial point 14)
- ✓ Time talk by visuals (e.g. 5 slides by 15 minute talk = 3 minutes per slide)

✓ Better to fall a little short of time allocation as you **will often** over run it

✓ Make sure your talk synchronises with the slide on view at any given point

✓ Project your voice so that everyone in the room can hear (direct your talk to the back row of the class)

✓ Do not stand motionless

✓ Spread eye contact around audience

✓ Map out where you are going and summarise main points at the end

✓ Have a practice run-through with friends

✓ Check out beforehand that all equipment works (such as OHP)

✓ Leave time for questions.

3.3	
essay writing tips	

Learning outcomes

By the end of this section you should be able to:

• Quickly engage with the main arguments

• Channel your passions constructively

• Note your main arguments in an outline

• Find and focus on your central topic questions

• Weave quotations into your essay

Getting into the flow

In essay writing one of your first aims should be to get your mind active and engaged with the subject of Criminal Justice. You can 'warm up' for your essay by tossing the ideas to and fro within your head before you begin to write ('brainstorming'). This will allow you to think within the framework of your topic, and this will be especially important if you are coming to the subject for the first time. You may wish to 'dictate' your thoughts on to a tape recorder or dictaphone.

The tributary principle

In an essay you should ensure that every idea you introduce is moving toward the overall theme you are addressing. Your ideas should 'flow' like a stream. Your idea might of course be relevant to a subheading that is in turn relevant to a main heading. Every idea you introduce is to be a 'feeder' into the flowing theme. You should never leave the reader or examiner trying to work out what the relevance of certain ideas or themes may have been. It is one thing to have grasped your subject thoroughly (use the **Running themes**) but quite another to convince your reader that this is the case. Your aim should be to build up ideas sentence-by-sentence and paragraph-by-paragraph, until you have communicated your clear purpose to the reader.

Write the essay topic in BIG letters on a sheet of paper and put this in front of you as you begin to write. This way you will not lose sight of the actual topic, problem or theme. It is important in essay writing that you do not only include material that is relevant, but that you also make the linking statements that show the connection to the reader. You may cite some learned sources or legal cases to back up your argument.

Listing and linking the key concepts (running themes)

All subjects will have central concepts; these can be usefully labelled by the **Running themes** presented in this text. You may also find the **Glossary of Criminal Justice and legal terms** useful in the appendices of this course companion. The central words or terms are the essential raw materials that you will need to build upon. Ensure that you learn the necessary words and their definitions, and that you can go on to link the key words together so that, in your learning activities, you will add understanding to your basic memory work.

It is useful to list your key words or running themes under general headings. You may not always see the connections immediately but when you later come back to a problem (or revise for the exam), you will find that your thinking is much clearer and has indeed changed.

Example: Write an essay on 'Youth and Crime'

You might decide to draft your outline points in the following manner (or you may prefer to use a mind map approach):

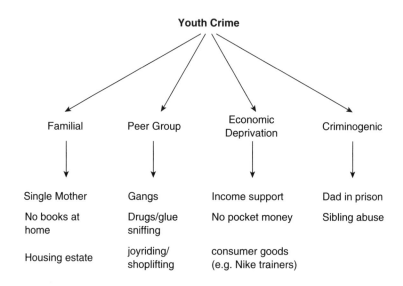

Youth Crime

Familial	Peer Group	Economic Deprivation	Criminogenic
Single Mother	Gangs	Income support	Dad in prison
No books at home	Drugs/glue sniffing	No pocket money	Sibling abuse
Housing estate	joyriding/ shoplifting	consumer goods (e.g. Nike trainers)	

Critical writing

In higher education, students are required to make the transition from descriptive to critical writing. If you can think of the critical (discursive) approach similar to a legal case that is being conducted in a criminal court, where there is both a prosecution and a defence, you then enter the critical or discursive argument. Your concern should be for objectivity, transparency and fairness, not subjectivity and giving your own opinion.

For example, no matter how passionately you may feel about a given cause (e.g. the Death Penalty), you must not allow information to be filtered out because of your personal prejudice. An essay is not to become a crusade for a cause in which the contrary arguments are not addressed in an even-handed manner. You should show awareness that opposite views are held and you should at least represent these as accurately as possible.

> *Your role as the essay writer is like that of a judge in that you must ensure that all the evidence is heard, and that nothing will compromise either party. Similar to the 'Disclosure Process' in court, where both the defence and the prosecution have to disclose their evidence to each other.*

Example of an issue that may stir up passions:

'Arguments for and against the re-introduction of the Death Penalty'
For

- For serial killers, paedophiles, rapists
- As a deterrent to society
- As a political tool (such as the 'law and order' debate)
- The 'will of the people'
- It works in some states/countries (Texas, Singapore)
- Cheaper than prisons – cost effective.

Against

- Human rights
- Humans should not liken themselves to God and judge upon fellow men
- Protecting the innocent
- Miscarriages of justice
- Long suffering (appeals) on Death Row (e.g. California – St Quentin Prison).

Structuring an essay outline

Whenever you sense a flow of inspiration to write on a given subject, it is essential that you put this into a structure (or essay plan) that will allow your inspiration to be communicated clearly. It is a basic principle in all walks of life that a good structure facilitates good communication. Therefore, when you have the flow of inspiration in your essay you must put this into a structure that will allow the marker to recognise the true quality of your work.

Your essay plan should have the following: An Introduction and a Conclusion, plus three main headings, which should have each of several subheadings. Once you have drafted this outline you can then easily sketch an Introduction, and you will have been well prepared for the Conclusion when you arrive at that point.

> *A good structure will help you balance the weight of each of your arguments against each other, and arrange your points in the order that will facilitate the fluent progression of your argument.*

Example: Write an essay that assesses the dynamics of a Magistrates' Bench when sentencing an offender who has been found (who has pleaded) guilty.

1 Consider the seriousness of the offence

    a. Are JPs sentencing powers appropriate?
    b. Has there been a timely guilty plea?
    c. Consider aggravating/mitigating factors of the offence.
    d. Impact on the victim.

2 Take preliminary view of seriousness, then consider offender mitigation

    a. Offence racially aggravated?
    b. Any previous convictions (antecedents)?
    c. Current offence linked to previous offence?
    d. Timely guilty plea or amends to victim? (RJ)

3 Decide on sentence

    a. Reduced sentence for timely guilty plea.
    b. Discount of up to one third (e.g. fine).
    c. Prison/fine/community sentence?
    d. Award of compensation to victim.

Finding major questions: the hypothesis

When you are constructing a draft outline for an essay or project, you should ask what the major question or questions are that you wish to address (this is often referred to as the 'hypothesis'). It would be useful to make a list of all the issues that spring to mind that you might wish to tackle. The ability to design a good question is an art form that should be cultivated, and such questions will allow you to impress your assessor with the quality of your thinking.

> *If you construct your ideas around key questions, this will help you focus your mind and engage effectively with your subject. Your role will be like that of a detective, or investigatory Magistrate, exploring the evidence and investigating the findings.*

If you were asked to write an essay about the effectiveness of the police in your local community you might pose the following questions as your starting point.

Example: The effectiveness of Community Police Support Officers (CPSOs) in the local community: initial questions.

- Is there a high profile police presence already?
- Are there regular 'beat' officers and patrol car activities?
- Do recent statistics show increases or decreases in crime in the area?
- What is the current involvement of police officers and CPSOs in your locality (e.g. Neighbourhood Watch; School Support and Awareness Training; Local Businesses; Pubs; Community Leaders etc)?
- Does the local community welcome and support the police/CPSOs?
- Do the police have a good reputation for responding to calls?
- Do the police harass people unnecessarily (e.g. stop and search)?
- How do local minority groups perceive the police?
- Do the police have an effective complaints procedure to deal with grievances against them?
- Do the police solicit and respond to local community concerns?
- How effective are local CPSOs and what are their powers under PACE?

Rest your case

It should be your aim to give the clear impression that your arguments are not based entirely on hunches, bias, feelings or intuition. In exams and essay questions it is usually assumed (even if not directly specified) that you will appeal to evidence to support your claims. Therefore, when you write your essay you should ensure that it is liberally sprinkled with citations and evidence from the learned literature known as sources. By the time the assessor (examiner) reaches the end of your work, s/he should be convinced that your conclusions are evidence based and most of all: that *you* did the research. A fatal flaw to be avoided is to make claims for which you have provided no authoritative source.

Give the clear impression that what you have asserted is derived from recognised (up-to-date) sources. It also looks impressive if you spread your citations across your essay rather than compressing them into a paragraph or two at the beginning or end.

Citing sources and evidencing your research

Example: Introducing your evidence and literature sources

- According to O'Neil (1999)...
- Wilson (2003) has concluded that...
- Taylor (2004) found that...
- It has been claimed by McKibben (2002) that...
- Appleby (2001) asserted that...
- A review of the evidence by Lawlor (2004) suggests that...
- Findings from a meta-analysis presented by Rea (2003) would indicate that...

You must always cite your sources; never pass passages from a book or the internet off as your own. Your examiner can tell!

Careful use of quotations (citations)

Although it is desirable to present a good range of cited sources, it is not judicious to present these as a 'patchwork quilt' – i.e. you just 'cut and paste' together what others have said with little thought for interpretative comment or coherent structure of your own making. It is a good general point to aim to avoid very lengthy quotes – short ones can be very effective (maximum two lines). Aim at blending the quotations as naturally as possible into the flow of your sentences. Also, it is good to vary your practices – sometimes use short, direct, brief quotes (cite page number as well as author and year at the end of the quote), and at times you can summarise the gist of a quote in your own words. In this case you should cite the author's name and year of publication but leave out quotation marks and page number.

> *Use your quotes (quotations) and evidence in a manner that demonstrates that you have thought the issue through, and have integrated them in a manner that shows you have been focused and selective in the use of your learned sources. Always put quotes in quotation marks and indent in the text.*

In terms of referencing, practice may vary from one discipline to the next, but some general points that will go a long way in contributing to good practice are:

- If a reference is cited in the text (or as footnotes/endnotes), it must also be in the bibliography (list of textbooks and journal articles) at the end (and vice-versa)
- Names and dates in text should correspond exactly with the list in your 'References' or 'Bibliography'
- List of References and Bibliography should be in alphabetical order by the surname (not the initials) of the author or first author
- Any reference you make in the text should be traceable by the reader (they should clearly be able to identify and trace the source)
- Internet sources: you must cite the full web-page (url) at the end of your References/Bibliography (see: 4.4 Internet sources).

A clearly defined Introduction

In an Introduction to an essay you have the opportunity to define the problem or issue that is being addressed and to set it within context. Resist the temptation to elaborate on any issue at the introductory stage. What you want to give in your Introduction is the theme (or 'overture' in musical terms) which is to provide a little taster of what will follow in order to stimulate the reader's (examiner's) appetite.

> *You may wish to write the Introduction last! This will then give a better definition of the problem and hypothesis. Some even leave the full title of their essay, project or dissertation to the end, and just use a 'working title' to start off with.*

Conclusion – adding the finishing touches

In the Conclusion you should aim to tie your essay together in a clear and coherent manner. You should summarise in a concise manner what you have said in the whole piece. It is a fact that most readers (examiners) will read the Introduction and then the Conclusion first, before they delve into the main part of your essay or dissertation. It is your last chance to leave an overall impression in your reader's mind. Therefore, you will at this stage want to do justice to your efforts and not sell yourself short. The Conclusion has to be the 'showpiece' of your whole essay or dissertation. This is your opportunity to identify where the strongest evidence points or where the balance of probability lies.

The Conclusion to an exam question often has to be written hurriedly under the pressure of time, but with an essay (course work) you have time to reflect on, refine and adjust the content to your satisfaction. It should be your goal to make the Conclusion a smooth finish that does justice to the range of content in summary and succinct form. Do not underestimate the value of an effective Conclusion. 'Sign off' your essay or project in a manner that brings closure to the treatment of your subject.

The Conclusion facilitates the chance to demonstrate where the findings have brought us to date, to highlight the issues that remain unresolved and to point to where future research should take us. Criminologists and Criminal Justice Specialists often finish with a question or further hypothesis ('...it remains to be seen...').

Checklist: Summary for essay writing

✓ Before you start, have a 'warm up' by tossing the issues around in your head (brainstorming)

✓ List the major concepts and link them in fluent form

✓ Design a structure (outline) that will facilitate balance, progression, fluency and clarity

✓ Pose questions (hypothesis) and address these in a critical fashion

✓ Demonstrate that your arguments rest on evidence and spread cited sources across your essay

✓ Provide an Introduction that sets the scene and a Conclusion that rounds off the arguments.

Checklist: Attempt to write (or at least think about) some additional features that would help facilitate good essay writing:

✓ ....

✓ ....

✓ ....

✓ ....

✓ ....

In the above checklist you could have features such as: originality; clarity in sentence and paragraph structure; applied aspects; addressing a subject you feel passionately about; and the ability to avoid going off on a tangent.

3.4	
revision hints and tips	

Learning outcomes

By the end of this section you should be able to:

- Map out your accumulated material for revision
- Choose summary tags to guide your revision
- Keep well-organised folders for revision
- Make use of effective memory techniques
- Revision that combines bullet points and in-depth reading
- Profit from the benefits of revising with others

- Attend to the practical exam revision workshops offered by your college/university
- Keep panic at bay
- Use strategies that keep you task-focused during the exam
- Select and apply relevant points from your prepared outlines.

The return journey

In a return journey you will usually pass by all the same places that you had already passed when you were outward bound. If you had observed the various landmarks on your outward journey you would be likely to remember them on your return. Similarly, RE-vision is a means to 'revisit' what you have encountered before. Familiarity with your material can help reduce anxiety, inspire confidence and fuel motivation for further learning and good performance.

If you are to capitalise on your revision period, then you must have your materials arranged and at hand for the time when you are ready to make your 'return' journey through all your notes.

Start at the beginning

Strategy for revision should be on your mind from your first lecture at the beginning of your academic semester. You should be like the squirrel that stores up nuts for the winter. Do not waste any lecture, tutorial, seminar, group discussion etc. by letting the material evaporate into thin air. Get into the habit of making a few guidelines for revision after each learning activity. Keep a folder, or file, or little notebook that is reserved for revision and write out the major points that you have learned. By establishing this regular practice you will find that what you have learned becomes consolidated in your mind, and you will also be in a better position to 'import' and 'export' your material both within and across subjects.

If you take revision notes regularly, and do not make the task too tedious, you will be amazed at how much useful summary material you have accumulated when revision time comes. Also, this is where your seminar/tutorial notes come in handy.

Compile summary notes

It would be useful and convenient to have a little notebook or (prompt) cards on which you can write outline summaries that provide you with an overview of your subject at a glance. You could also use treasury tags to hold different batches of cards together whilst still allowing for inserts and re-sorting. Such practical resources can easily be slipped into your pocket or bag and produced when you are on the bus or train or whilst sitting in a traffic jam. They would also be useful if you are standing in a queue or waiting for someone who is not in a rush! A glance over your notes will consolidate your learning and will also activate your mind to think further about your subject. Therefore it would also be useful to make note of the questions that you would like to think about in greater depth. Your primary task is to get into the habit of constructing outline notes that will be useful for revision, and a worked example is provided below.

> *There is a part of the mind that will continue to work on problems when you have moved on to focus on other issues. Therefore, if you feed on useful, targeted information, your mind will continue to work on 'auto-pilot' after you have 'switched off'.*

Example: Part of a course on the Criminal Justice System and the Criminal Process is on 'the problem of crime'.

Your outline revision structure for this might be as follows:

1 Defining crime

- What is crime?
- What is meant by 'law violation'?
- What's the difference between the violation of the law and moral codes?
- What is deviance?

2 Types of crime

- Social crime
- Economic crime
- White collar crime
- Terrorism
- Youth crime
- Gender crime
- Hate crime

- Physical or mental abuse
- Cybercrime.

3 Systems of crime control

- Police force
- Criminal courts
- Prosecution and punishment
- Community solutions
- Youth justice.

Keep organised records

People who have a fulfilled career have usually developed the twin skills of time and task management. It is worth pausing to remember that you can use your academic training to prepare for your future career in this respect. Therefore, ensure that you do not fall short of your potential because these qualities have not been cultivated. One important tactic is to keep a folder for each subject and divide this topic-by-topic. You can keep your topics in the same order in which they are presented in your course lectures or in the contents pages of Part 2 of this course companion (e.g. police; Magistrates; prisons; probation etc). Bind them together in a ring binder or folder and use subject dividers to keep them apart. Make a numbered list of the contents at the beginning of the folder, and list each topic clearly as it marks a new section in your folder.

Another important practice is to place all your notes on a given topic within the appropriate section and don't put off this simple task, do it straight away. Notes may come from lectures, seminars, tutorials, Internet searches, personal notes etc. It is also essential when you remove these for consultation that you return them to their 'home' immediately after use.

Academic success has as much to do with good organisation, planning and time management, as it has to do with ability. The value of the quality material you have accumulated on your academic programme may be diminished because you have not organised (filed) it into an easily retrievable form.

Use past papers

Revision will be very limited if it is confined to memory work. You should by all means read over your revision cards or notebook and keep the picture of the major facts in front of your mind's eye. What is important (at least two weeks before an examination) is that you apply yourself to actual (past) exam questions. It is essential that you become familiar with previous (past) exam papers, so that you will have some idea of how the questions are likely to be framed, how they are structured and the time frame you are given to answer the questions in. Therefore, build up a good range of past exam papers (especially recent ones) and add these to your folder.

If you think over previous exam questions, and write the answers down, this will help you not only recall what you have deposited in your memory, but also to develop your understanding of the issues. The questions from past exam papers, and further questions that you have developed yourself (or taken from tutorials) will allow you to 'chew the cud'.

You will have also noticed that the word 'evaluate' is in some exam questions. Whenever you see this in a question (or sometimes the question will end with 'Discuss'), your mind must go to work on making judgements ('pros' and 'cons'). You may decide to work through problems first and then through pleasures, or it may be your preference to compare point by point as you go along. Whatever conclusion you come to may be down to personal subjective preference but at least you will have worked through all the issues from both standpoints. The lesson is to ensure that part of your revision should include critical thinking as well as memory work.

Employ effective mnemonics (memory aids)

The Greek word from which *mnemonics* is derived refers to a tomb – a structure that is built in memory of a loved one, friend or respected person. 'Mnemonics' can be simply defined as aids to memory – devices that will help you recall information that might otherwise be difficult to retrieve from memory.

Visualisation is one technique that can be used to aid memory. For example, the location method is where a familiar journey is visualised and you can 'place' the facts that you wish to remember at various landmarks along the journey, e.g. a bus stop, a car park, a shop, a store, a bend, a police station, a traffic light etc. This has the advantage of making an association of the information you have to learn with other material that is already firmly embedded and structured in your memory. Therefore, once the relevant memory is activated, a dynamic 'domino effect' will be triggered. In memorising legal cases, you may put a short 'tag' on to each case.

Example: Memorising the date of criminal case law

<u>R v Woollin</u> [1999] House of Lords
Even if you do not get the *exact* date of the case, it is important to roughly get the era right and the socio-legal context when the case (or crime) took place. In an exam, examiners tend to let you get away with the approximate date of a legal case; in the case of *Woollin*, you may write'… the case took place in the late 1990s and the final judgement was heard in the House of Lords'.

Example: Memorising the date of Acts of Parliament

With Acts of Parliament (e.g. *Crime and Disorder Act 1998* or the *Criminal Justice Act 2003*) you must get the date absolutely right.

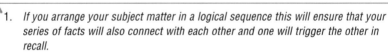

1. *If you arrange your subject matter in a logical sequence this will ensure that your series of facts will also connect with each other and one will trigger the other in recall.*
2. *You can use memory devices either at the stage of initial learning (like tape-recording legal cases) or when you later return to consolidate.*

Location method

Visualisation – turn information into pictures.

Alliteration's artful aid – Find a series of words that all begin with the same letter. The educationalist Ebbinghaus suggests the learning process of remembering by alliteration, such as: Recall, Recognition, Reconstruction and Re-learning. He uses alliteration as a confidence booster because it demonstrates that memory is more powerful than is often imagined.

Peg system – 'Hang' information onto a term so that when you hear the term you will remember the ideas connected with it (an umbrella term). In the example on 'youth and crime' there are four different types: Familial; Peer Group; Economic Deprivation and Criminogenic. Under 'familial' you could remember: single mother; no books at home; housing estate etc (see p. 146 for an example).

Hierarchical system – This is a development of the previous point with higher-order, middle-order and lower-order terms. For example you could think of the continents of the world (higher-order), and then group these into the countries under them (middle-order). Under countries you could have cities, rivers and mountains (lower-order).

Acronyms – Take the first letter of all the key words and make a word form these. An example from business is SWOT – Strengths, Weaknesses, Opportunities and Threats.

Mind maps – These have become very popular – they allow you to draw lines that stretch out from the central idea and to develop the subsidiary ideas in the same way. It is a little like the pegging and hierarchical methods combined and turned sideways! The method has the advantage of giving you the complete picture at a glance, although they can become a complex work of art! An example given above was the one with 'Youth Crime' and its arrows (see p. 146).

Rhymes and chimes – words that rhyme and words that end with a similar sound (e.g. commemoration, celebration, anticipation). These provide another dimension to memory work by including sound. Memory can be enhanced when information is processed in various modalities, for example, hearing, seeing, speaking, visualising.

In summary, you should work at finding the balance between these learning methods. Your outline revision or 'prompt' cards might be best reserved for short bus journeys, whereas extended reading might be better employed for longer revision slots at home or in the library. Your ultimate goal should be to bring together an effective, working approach that will enable you to face your exam questions comprehensively and confidently.

1. *In revision it is useful to alternate between scanning over your outline points, and reading through your notes, articles, chapters etc in an in-depth manner.*
2. *Use different times, places and methods that will provide you with variety when you revise. This will prevent monotony and facilitate freshness.*
3. *Use your taped material and listen to it, e.g. in the car, in the gym etc (going to sleep with it will not work!).*

Revising with others

If you can find a few other students to revise with, this will provide another fresh approach to the last stages of your learning. Firstly ensure that others carry their workload and are not merely using the hard work of others (you!) as a short cut to success. Of course you should think of group sessions as one of the strings on your violin, but not the only string. This collective approach would allow you to assess your strengths and weaknesses (showing you where you are off track), and benefit from the resources and insights of others. Before you meet up you can each design some questions for the whole group to address. The group could also go through past exam papers and discuss the points that might provide an effective response to each question. It should not be the aim of the group to provide standard and identical answers for each group member to mimic.

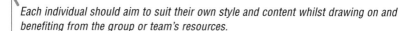

Each individual should aim to suit their own style and content whilst drawing on and benefiting from the group or team's resources.

Checklist: Good study habits for revision time

✓ Set a date for the 'official' beginning of revision and prepare for 'revision mode' (use calendar or year-planner)

✓ Do not force cramming by leaving revision too late (take leave from work if necessary)

✓ Take breaks from revision to avoid saturation

✓ Indulge in relaxing activities to give your mind a break from pressure (do some sport; take dog for a walk; watch some TV – unrelated to your study)

✓ Minimise or eliminate use of alcohol during the revision season

✓ Get into a good rhythm of sleep to allow renewal of your mind

✓ Avoid excessive caffeine especially at night so that sleep is not disrupted (try some herbal teas!)

✓ Try to adhere to regular eating patterns

✓ Try and get some fresh air each day

✓ Avoid excessive dependence on junk food and snacks.

Checklist: Write your own checklist on what you add to the revision process to ensure it is not just a memory exercise.

✓ ....

✓ ....

✓ ....

✓ ....

✓ ....

In the above checklist, what you could add to memory work during revision might include using past exam papers, setting problem-solving tasks, doing drawings to show connections and directions between various concepts, explaining concepts to student friends in joint revision sessions, or devising your own mock exam questions.

3.5	
exam tips	

Learning outcomes

By the end of this section you should be able to:

- Develop strategies for controlling your nervous energy
- Tackle worked examples of time and task management in exams
- Attend to the practical details associated with the exam
- Stay focused on the exam questions
- Link revision outlines to strategy for addressing exam questions.

Handling your nerves

Exam nerves are not unusual and it has been concluded that test anxiety arises because of the perception that your performance is being evaluated, that the consequences are likely to be serious and that you are working under the pressure of a time restriction. If you focus on the task at hand rather than on feeding a downward negative spiral in your thinking patterns, this will help you keep your nerves under control. In the run up to your exams you can practise some simple relaxation techniques that will help you bring stress under control. If you have sufficiently revised and practised with your past exam papers, you ought to 'look forward' to getting into the exam room in order to empty 'your C-Drive'!

It is a very good thing if you can interpret your nervous reactions positively, *but the symptoms are more likely to be problematic if you interpret them negatively. If you pay too much attention to them, or allow them to interfere with your exam preparation or performance, you will become more nervous.*

Practices that may help reduce or buffer the effects of exam stress

- Listening to music
- Going for a brisk walk or doing exercise
- Simple breathing exercises
- Joining a yoga class
- Some muscle relaxation or stretching exercises
- Watching a movie
- Enjoying some laughter
- Relaxing in a bath (with aroma-oils, candles, music etc).

The best choice is going to be the one (or combination) that works best for you – perhaps to be discovered by trial and error. Some of the above techniques can be practised on the morning of the exam, and even the memory of them can be used just before the exam. The idea behind all this is, firstly, stress levels must come down, and secondly, relaxing thoughts will serve to displace stressful reactions.

1. *It is important you are convinced that your stress levels can come under control, and that you can have a say in this*
2. *Do not give anxiety a chance!*
3. *Do not meet up with people (especially just before going into the exam) that stress you out; they might tell you about a new topic you may not have revised.*

Time management with examples

The all-important matter as you approach an exam is to develop the belief that you can take control of the situation. One of the issues you will need to be clear about before the exam is the length of time you should allocate to each question. Sometimes this can be quite simple (although it is always necessary to read the rubric carefully), for example, if two questions are to be answered in a two-hour paper, you should allow one hour for each question. If it is a two-hour paper with one essay question and five shorter answers, you could allow one hour for the essay and 12 minutes each for the shorter questions. However, you always need to check the weighting for the marks on each question, and you will also need to deduct whatever time it takes you to read over the paper and to choose your questions. See if you can work out a time management strategy in each of the following scenarios. More importantly, give yourself some practice on the papers you are likely to face.

1. *Remember to check if the structure of your exam paper is the same as on previous years (ask your lecturer/tutor about this)*
2. *Check the time allowed on the exam paper (e.g. two hours plus 15 minutes' reading tim)*
3. *Make sure you divide your time equally between questions (usually you'll need about 25–30 minutes for one question) – leave adequate time at the end of the exam for reading through the whole paper, to check for spelling, grammar and style (usually 10 minutes)*
4. *Do not spend longer on your 'strongest' questions and answer. Use the cut-off time (e.g. 30 minutes) in order to go on to the next question*
5. *Make sure you read the question properly!*
6. *Ensure that you have read the introductory rubric to the exam paper and each new section carefully in the exam.*

EXERCISE

Examples for working out the division of exam answer-time

1. **A three-hour paper with four compulsory questions (equally weighted in marks)**

2. **A three-hour paper with two essays and ten short questions (each of the three sections carry one third of the marks)**

3. **A two-hour paper with two essay questions and 100 multiple-choice questions (half the marks are on the two essays and the other half of the marks on the multiple choice section).**

1. *Get into the calculating frame of mind and be sure to have the calculations done before the exam (e.g. exact time allocation – if a paper is two and a half hours long and you have to answer three essay questions)*
2. *Ensure that the structure of the exam has not changed since last year (especially with a new course lecturer)*
3. *Deduct the time taken to read over the paper in allocating time to each question (unless there is additional reading time).*

Suggested answers to previous exercise: Division of exam answer time

1. This allows 45 minutes for each question (4 questions × 45 minutes = 2 hours). However, if you allow 40 minutes for each question this will give you 20 minutes (4 questions × 5 minutes) to read over the paper and plan your outlines.

2. In this example you can spend 1 hour on each of the two major questions, and 1 hour on the ten short questions. For the two major questions you could allow 10 minutes for reading and planning on each, and 50 minutes for writing. In the ten short questions, you could allow 6 minutes in total for each (10 questions × 6 minutes = 60 minutes). However, if you allow approximately 1 minute reading and planning time, this will allow 5 minutes writing time for each question.

3. In this case you have to divide 120 minutes by three questions – this allows 40 minutes for each. You could, for example, allow 5 minutes reading/planning time for each essay and 35 minutes for writing (or 10 minutes reading/planning and 30 minutes writing). After you have completed the two major questions you are left with 40 minutes to tackle the 100 multiple-choice questions.

1. *Keeping awareness of time limitations will help you write succinctly*
2. *Keeping focused on the task will prevent you dressing up your responses with unnecessary padding (waffle).*

Some students put as much effort into their rough work as they do into their exam essay. Do NOT do this!

Attend to practical details

This short section is designed to remind you of the practical details that should be attended to in preparation for an exam. There are always students who turn up late, go to the wrong venue, attend the wrong exam, or do not turn up at all! Check and re-check that you have all the details of each exam (room or location) correctly noted. What you don't need is to arrive late and then have to tame your panic reactions. The exam season is the time when you should aim to be at your best.

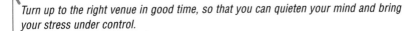

Turn up to the right venue in good time, so that you can quieten your mind and bring your stress under control.

Make note of the following details and check that you have taken control of each one.

Checklist: Practical exam details

✓ Check that you have the correct venue
✓ Make sure you know how to locate the venue before the exam day
✓ Ensure that the exam time you have noted is accurate
✓ Allow sufficient time for your journey and consider the possibility of delays
✓ Bring an adequate supply of stationary and include back up
✓ Bring a watch/clock for your time and task management
✓ You may need a small bottle of still water
✓ You may need to bring some tissues
✓ Observe whatever exam regulations your university/college has set in place
✓ Bring your student ID card (you may need to fill in required personal details before the exam begins).

Control wandering thoughts

In a simple study conducted in the 1960s, Ganzer found that students who frequently lifted their heads and looked away from their scripts during exams tended to perform poorly. This makes sense because it implies that the students were taking too much time out when they should have been on task.

Practical suggestions for controlling wandering thoughts

1.   Be aware that this problem is detrimental to performance
2.   Do not look around to find distractions
3.   If distracted, write down 'keep focused on task'
4.   If distracted again, look back at the above and continue to do this
5.   Start to draft rough work as soon as you can
6.   If you struggle with initial focus then re-read or elaborate on your rough work
7.   If you have commenced your essay re-read your last paragraph
8.   Do not throw fuel on your distracting thoughts – starve them by re-engaging with the task at hand.

1.   Although you may have clear templates with a definite structure or framework for organising your material, you will need to be flexible about how this should be applied to your exam questions. Do not learn 'template' essays off by heart!
2.   Restrict your material to what is relevant to the question, but bear in mind that this may allow you some scope.

The art of 'name dropping'

In most topics at university or college, you will be required to cite studies as evidence for your arguments and to link these to the names of researchers, scholars or theorists. It will help if you can use the correct dates or at least the decades, and it is good to demonstrate that you have used contemporary sources, and have done some independent work. An examiner will have dozens if not hundreds of scripts to work through and they will know if you are just repeating the same phrases from the same sources as everyone else. There is inevitably a certain amount of this that must go on, but there is room for you to add fresh and original touches that demonstrate independence and imagination.

1.   Give a clear impression that you have done more than the bare minimum of research and that you have enthusiasm for the subject
2.   Spread the use of researchers' or learned academics' names across your exam essay (or project), rather than compressing them into, for example, only the Introduction or the last paragraph.

3.6	
tips on interpreting essay and exam questions	

Learning outcomes

By the end of this section you should be able to:

- Focus on the issues that are relevant and central
- Read questions carefully and take account of all the words
- Produce a balanced critique in your outline structures
- Screen for the key words that will shape your response
- Focus on different shades of meaning between 'critique', 'evaluate', 'discuss' and 'compare and contrast'.

Although examiners do not deliberately design questions to trick you or trip you up, they cannot always prevent you from seeing things that were not designed to be there.

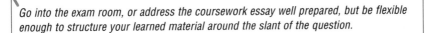

Go into the exam room, or address the coursework essay well prepared, but be flexible enough to structure your learned material around the slant of the question.

A politician's answer

Politicians are renowned for refusing to answer questions directly or for evading them through raising other questions. A humorous example is when a politician was asked, 'Is it true that you always answer questions by asking another?', the reply given was, 'Who told you that?'. Therefore, make sure that you answer the set question, although there may be other questions that arise out of this for further study that you might want to highlight in your Conclusion. As a first principle you must answer the set question and not another question that you had hoped for in the exam or essay.

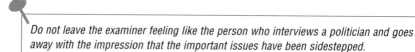

Do not leave the examiner feeling like the person who interviews a politician and goes away with the impression that the important issues have been sidestepped.

Example: What are children sent to prison for? Discuss the relevant criminal offences, youth legislation and current penal policy trends.

Directly relevant points

- 12–14-year-olds sent to custody
- Violent offences
- ss 73–79 CDA 1998
- Types of sentences
- Time spent in custody must be constructive
- Throughcare arrangements
- Youth Justice Board.

Less relevant points

- Local authority units
- ASBOs
- Types of establishments (YOIs)
- Causes of crime
- Familial background.

Although some of the points listed in the 'less relevant' list may be relevant to the causes of youthful offending, they are not as directly relevant to youth imprisonment today and penal policy. Do pay attention to the full question which is asked of you, and don't learn a pre-prepared essay topic off by heart which is not at all relevant to the question and issues that should be addressed. Some of the points in the 'less relevant' list above therefore could be mentioned briefly, but do not go off on a tangent.

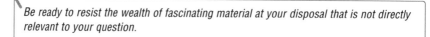

Be ready to resist the wealth of fascinating material at your disposal that is not directly relevant to your question.

Missing your question

A student bitterly complained after an exam that the topic he had revised so thoroughly had not been tested in the exam. The first response to that is that students should always cover enough topics to avoid selling themselves short in the exam – the habit of 'question spotting' is always a risky game to play. However, the reality in the anecdotal example was that the question the student was looking for was there, but he had not seen it. He had expected the question to be couched in certain words and he could not find these when he scanned over the questions in blind panic. Maybe he had only revised with one particular past exam paper, and was looking for that very wording. The simple lesson therefore, is always *read over the questions carefully*, slowly and thoughtfully. This practice is time well spent.

1. You can miss the question if you restrict yourself to looking for a set form of words (e.g. those used in past exam papers)
2. You must read over all the words in the exam question carefully.

Write it down

You may not have the time to write the question down in the exam, but you could perhaps quietly articulate it with your lips. Think of how easy it is to misunderstand a question that has been put to you verbally because you have misinterpreted the tone or emphasis.

1. If you read over the question several times you should be aware of all the key words and will begin to sense the connections between the ideas
2. Read each question (whisper it) quietly to yourself
3. You should then envisage the possible directions you should take in your response/s. Write brief bullet points down in 'rough'.

Pursue a critical approach

In degree courses you are usually expected to write *critically* rather than merely descriptively, although it may be necessary to use some minimal descriptive substance as the raw material for your debate.

Example: What is Community Punishment? Has the Probation Service failed in its duty? Discuss and evaluate recent evidence.

Arguments for the success of the Probation Service

- Reduce reoffending
- New ways of community punishment (community sentence)
- Increased responsibilities
- Protection of the public
- Victim–offender mediation (RS).

Arguments against

- Changing role of the Probation Officer (since 2000)
- Probation Officer as the 'enforcer and punisher'
- No longer rehabilitative support of offenders
- Increased prosecutions for bail offences
- Form-filling and managerialism.

Given that the question is about a critical evaluation of the evidence (i.e. changing role of the National Probation Service), you would need to address the issues one by one from both standpoints. What you should not do is digress into a tangent about the physical characteristics of a Probation Officer, nor go into the role of the Prison Service at this point. Neither should you be drawn into a lengthy description of offending behaviour patterns, nor how criminals are arrested by the police.

Analyse the parts

A good essay cannot be constructed without reference to the parts. Given the example of writing about the changing role of the Probation Service in recent years, you need source evidence to support your argument, such as HM Inspector of Probation Reports (since 2000), online research into the National Probation Service and journal articles by learned academics.

Furthermore, the parts will arise as you break down the question into the components it suggests to you. Although the breaking down of a question into components is not sufficient for an excellent essay, it is a necessary starting point.

To achieve a good response to an exam or essay/assignment-type question, aim to integrate the individual issues presented in a manner that gives shape and direction to your efforts.

Example: Comment and evaluate the current jury system of England and Wales. Evaluate the advantages and disadvantages.

This is a straightforward question in that you have two major sections – advantages and disadvantages. You are left with the choice of the issues that you wish to address, and you can arrange these in the order you prefer. Your aim should be to ensure that you do not have a lopsided view of this even if you feel quite strongly one way or the other.

Example: In a critical manner, trace western society's changing attitudes to the death penalty.

In this case you might want to consider the role of governments, the abolition of the death penalty in England in 1965 and why other countries (e.g. China, Russia or California) have kept capital punishment as the ultimate penal sanction a state has over a human being. Comment on how the death penalty fits with the *European Convention on Human Rights* and human rights legislation in England (e.g. *Human Rights Act 1998*). However, you will need to have some reference points to the past as you are asked to address the issue of change. There would also be scope to look at where the strongest influences for change arise and where the strongest resistance comes from. You might argue that the changes have been dramatic or evolutionary.

Give yourself plenty of practice at thinking of questions in this kind of way and use past papers.

When asked to discuss

Students often ask how much of their own opinion they should include in an essay. In a discussion your aim should be not just to identify and define all the parts that contribute, but also to show where they fit (or don't fit) into the overall picture.

1. *Although the word 'discuss' implies some allowance for your opinion, remember that this should be informed opinion rather than groundless speculation*
2. *Don't inform your 'learned opinion' only by what you read in the popular tabloid press*
3. *There must be direction, order, structure and an end project with a reasoned conclusion.*

Checklist: Features of a response to a 'discuss' question

✓ Contains a chain of issues that lead into each other in sequence
✓ Clear shape and direction is unfolded in the progression of the argument
✓ Underpinned by reference to findings and certainties
✓ Identification of issues where doubt remains
✓ Tone of argument may be tentative but should not be vague.

If a critique is requested

One example that might help clarify what is involved in a critique is the already mentioned and hotly debated topic of the *reintroduction of capital punishment*. It would be important, in the interest of balance and fairness, to present all sides and shades of the argument. You would then look at whether there is available evidence to support each argument, and you might introduce issues that have been coloured by prejudice, tradition, religion and legislation. It would be an aim to identify emotional arguments, arguments based on intuition and to get down to those arguments that really have solid evidence-based support. Finally you would want to flag up where the strongest evidence appears to lie, and you should also identify issues that appear to be inconclusive. It would be expected that you should, if possible, arrive at some certainties.

Checklist: Write your own summary checklist for the features of a critique. You can either summarise the above points, or use your own points or a mixture of the two.

✓ ....
✓ ....
✓ ....
✓ ....
✓ ....

If asked to compare and contrast

When asked to compare and contrast, you should be thinking in terms of similarities and differences. You should ask what the two issues share in common, and what features of each are distinct. Your preferred strategy for tackling this might be to firstly work through all the similarities and then through all the contrasts (or vice-versa). On the other hand, work through a similarity and a contrast, followed by another similarity and contrast etc.

Example: Compare and contrast 'Retribution' and 'Restorative Justice' (RJ) as punishment and sentencing principles.

Similarities

- Formal justice principles
- Used in sentencing guidelines
- Both are social justice principles
- Both are linked to due process
- Human rights elements
- Punishment must fit the crime.

Contrasts

- The guilty must be punished (retribution)
- The guilty must be rehabilitated (RJ)
- Differences in sentencing outcomes
- Addresses future behaviour of criminal (RJ) vs. past criminal offending.

When you compare and contrast you should aim to paint a true picture of the full 'landscape'.

Whenever evaluation is requested

You have been given the task of evaluating the new sentencing powers of Magistrates under the *Criminal Justice Act 2003*. In your task you might want to review past features (retrospective), outline present features (perspective) and envisage positive future changes (prospective) in relation to Magistrates' Courts and their sentencing (e.g. sending someone to prison for 12 instead of 6 months or using increased 'community sentence' powers). This illustration may provoke you to think about how you might approach a question that asks you to evaluate some theory or concept in your own academic field of study.

Summary points: the *evaluation process*

- Has the theory/concept stood the test of time?
- Is there a supportive evidence base that would not easily be overturned?
- Are there questionable elements that have been or should be challenged?
- Does more recent evidence point to a need for modification?
- Is the theory/concept robust and likely to be around for the foreseeable future?
- Could it be strengthened through being merged with other theories/concepts?

It should be noted that the words presented in the above examples might not always be the exact words that will appear on your exam script, for example, you might find 'analyse', or 'outline' or 'investigate' etc. The best advice is to check over your past exam papers and familiarise yourself with the words that are most recurrent.

part four

additional resources

4.1

chronology of crime events

1953 – 19-year-old Derek Bentley is hanged, after being involved in the shooting of a policeman. His aunt campaigned for many years, and Bentley was finally granted a posthumous pardon in 1999.

1955 – 13 July: 28-year-old Ruth Ellis is the last woman to be hanged in England (Holloway Prison).

1963 – The Great Train Robbery. On 8 August a 20-man gang steal £2.6m in used bank notes from a Royal Mail train.

1965 – Abolition of the Death Penalty in Britain, substituted by a 'life imprisonment' sentence.

1966 – Moors murderers Ian Brady and Myra Hindley receive life sentences for the murder of four children on Saddleworth Moor. Hindley died November 2002 from a severe chest infection. She was one of the 'natural lifers' in prison.

1968 – Reggie and Ronald Kray (the Kray Twins) get a life sentence for the murder of gangsters George Cornell and Jack 'the Hat' McVitie.

1968 – Ten-year-old 'Mary Bell' is convicted of the murder of two little boys by strangulation, aged three and four, in Newcastle upon Tyne. The story is told by Gitta Sereny in *Cries Unheard: The Story of Mary Bell* (1998). Mary Bell was tried as an adult, found guilty of double murder and sentenced to 'life' imprisonment under Her Majesty's Pleasure (HMP).

1973 – Wendy Sewell is murdered in Bakewell, leading to the wrongful conviction of Stephen Downing, who spent 27 years in prison, before being released.

1974 – Lord Lucan vanishes after the murder of the nanny of his three children.

1975 – The body of Lesley Whittle, a 17-year-old heiress kidnapped from her Shropshire home 52 days earlier, is found at the bottom of a drain shaft. In June 1976, Donald Neilson, a builder from Bradford, is given five life sentences for her murder.

1979 – Jeremy Thorpe, former leader of the Liberal Party, is cleared of attempted murder. He was alleged to have plotted the demise of Norman Scott, who caused Thorpe to resign in 1976 over rumours of a homosexual affair.

1981 – Peter Sutcliffe, known as 'The Yorkshire Ripper', is sentenced to life imprisonment at the Old Bailey for the murder of 13 women.

1983 – Dennis Nilsen is charged with the murder of 12 men after human remains are found in his home in North London.

1985 – Autumn: the Brixton Riots break out, predominantly against the police. One person is killed, 50 injured and over 200 arrested.

1987 – The Hungerford Massacre. On 19 August, Michael Ryan goes on a rampage in Hungerford, Berkshire, shooting dead 16 people before turning the gun on himself. He was apparently motivated by 'Rambo' films.

1989 – 15 April: Hillsborough football stadium disaster. Sheffield Wednesday play Liverpool FC in the FA cup semi-final. 96 people die by being crushed to death at the old Sheffield stadium. Countless others are left mentally and physically injured, leading to long-standing legal challenges.

1993 – 22 April: the black 17-year-old A-Level student Stephen Lawrence is murdered in Eltham, East London.

1993 – February: two 10-year-old boys, Robert Thompson and Jon Venables, kill the toddler Jamie Bulger. November: Thompson and Venables (then 11) are tried and found guilty for murdering Jamie Bulger at Preston Crown Court.

1994 – Fred and Rosemary West are charged with the murders of 12 young women, including their daughter Heather. On 1 January 1995, Fred West hangs himself in Birmingham Prison. In October 1995 Rose West is sentenced to life imprisonment for 10 counts of murder and is one of the 'natural lifers' in the system.

1995 – 'Rogue Trader' Nick Leeson is arrested in Singapore after he bankrupted his own bank, Barings Bank and is charged with fraud. He gambled some the bank's assets of some £800m on the stock exchange. He served five years in Singapore's prison, and was extradited to Britain due to ill health.

1996 – The Dunblane Massacre. Lone gunman Thomas Hamilton kills 16 children and their teacher at a school in Dunblane, Scotland. Gun control legislation is put in place.

1997 – Sex Offender Register comes into force. It requires that some 12,000 convicted sex offenders at that time go on the (police and social services) register with their names and addresses.

1999 – Jill Dando, the TV and BBC Crimewatch Presenter, is murdered on the doorstep of her own home in Fulham, London on 26 April. Barry George, Dando's stalker, is found guilty of her murder in July 2001.

2000 – January: Harold Shipman, a GP, is found guilty on 15 counts of murder of his patients. He is to that date the UK's most prolific killer. A public inquiry discovers a further 215 patients lost their lives in Shipman's hands. He committed suicide in his prison cell in 2002.

2000 – March: Zahid Mubarek, a 19-year-old convicted criminal from East London, is killed on the eve of his release from Feltham Young Offenders' Institution when his white racist cellmate battered him to death with a table leg. A public inquiry into his death was held in 2005.

2000 – July: 8-year-old Sarah Payne's body is found in Sussex. In December 2001 Roy Whiting was found guilty and sentenced to life imprisonment. Trial judge Mr Justice Richard Curtis recommends that Whiting should serve a 'natural' life sentence where 'life' should mean life.

2000 – The *Human Rights Act 1998* comes into force on 2 October. The HRA is hailed as one of the most significant changes to British law since the Magna Carta. It enshrines the European Convention on Human Rights and Fundamental Freedoms (The Convention) in UK law.

2000 – November: 10-year-old Damilola Taylor from Nigeria is found bleeding to death on a housing estate in Peckham, South London. Two teenage boys (17-year-old twins with Southern European origin) are acquitted during their murder trial in June 2002, because the testimony of a key witness (girl 'Bromley' aged 13) was unreliable and discredited.

2001 – The carers (one of them her aunt) of Victoria Climbié, aged 8, are found guilty of her murder by child abuse. A number of inquiries follow into the duties of care of London Social Services.

2001 – Jamie Bulger's killers, Thompson and Venables (after turning 18) are released from secure youth custody and do not have to transfer to an adult prison, following Lord Chief Justice Woolf's direction. Both are given new identities and a life-long ban (anonymity order by the Family Court Division) now exists on their identities and whereabouts. No 'world' media is permitted to report on the young men.

2002 – 24 April: the body of missing 13-year-old Amanda (Millie) Dowler is found in the river Thames, near Walton on Thames. Her killer has not been found.

2002 – David Blunkett announces his intention to reclassify cannabis to class C, a category which does not have an automatic power of arrest for simple possession.

2002 – The remains of the two 10-year-old schoolgirls, Holly Wells and Jessica Chapman, are found near their homes in Soham, Cambridgeshire in September. The school caretaker Ian Huntley stands trial for their murder in October 2003, and is found guilty in December 2003. His girl-friend Maxine Carr stands trial at the same time for perverting the course of justice (lying on his behalf) and is found guilty. She is released from prison in 2004 and given a new identity. A lifelong anonymity order exists on her identity and whereabouts.

2002 – Honour Killing of 16-year-old Kurdish Heshu Yones in Acton, West London. Her attacker is her father Abdullah who stabbed his daughter 11 times and then slit her throat. Reasons were that he disapproved of her western dress and her Christian boyfriend.

2003 – Charlene Ellis (18) and Latisha Shakespeare (17) are gunned down outside a Birmingham hair salon in Aston. They were shot 'by mistake', resulting from a feud between two local gangs. Charlene's half-brother Marcus Elliss (24), Michael Gregory (22), Nathan Martin (26) and Rodrigo Simms (20) were convicted of their murder and given a life sentence each after a six-month Leicester Crown court trial in March 2005. The trial was marred by serious attempts to intimidate key witnesses.

2003 – December: Ian Huntley a primary school caretaker is convicted of the murder of two 10-year-old girls in Soham, Cambridgeshire: Holly Wells and Jessica Chapman.

2004 – 19 August, French woman Amelie Delagrange, 22, is found bludgeoned to death in Twickenham, London. The killer has not been found.

2004 – December: A Sikh father is found guilty of hiring a hitman to carry out the 'Honour Kllings' of his daughter Sanjit, 23, her Jewish boyfriend, Temple Jazac, 43, and Malcolm Calver, a man he mistook for Mr Jazac's father, on 26 September 2003.

2005 – Mary-Ann Leneghan (16) is stabbed in the neck and left to die in a Reading Park. November 2005, Old Bailey: six men, aged between 18 and 23, are charged with her murder and attempted murder of her friend, and the kidnap, rape and grievous bodily harm of both girls.

2005 – Bluewater Shopping Centre in Kent announces 'hoodies' ban. The guidelines say intimidating behaviour by groups or individuals and the wearing of clothing which deliberately obscures the face, such as hooded tops or baseball caps, will not be allowed.

2005 – 7 July: Four explosions rip across central London transport (No. 30 bus and various underground trains) at 8.50am on Thursday 7 July. At least 55 people are killed and 700 are injured in the blasts. Four suicide bombers died. Al-Quaida claims responsibility. Four further attacks on London transport follow a week later during lunchtime of 21 July.

4.2

glossary of legal terms

A

Abscond
Fail to surrender to bail, or leave the court/ police station before being dealt with. Also failure to return to prison after home leave.

Accused
The person charged. The person who has allegedly committed the offence.

Accredited programme
Community/prison programme approved by Prison and Probation Services or NOMS (see NOMS).

Acquittal
Discharge of defendant following verdict or direction of not guilty.

Act
As an Act of Parliament; Statute; law.

Actual Bodily Harm (ABH)
It is an offence contrary to s 47 of the *Offences Against the Person Act 1861* (OAPA) to commit an assault occasioning actual bodily harm. The *actus reus* (see *Actus reus*) of the offence consists of the *actus reus* for an assault or a battery plus a requirement that actual bodily harm is caused. The expression 'actual bodily harm' includes 'any harm...which interferes with the health or comfort of the victim' (see also GBH).

Actus Reus
Guilty act. The actions in the offence of which the defendant is accused: '*Actus non facit reum, nisi mens sit rea*' (an act does not make a person legally guilty unless the mind is legally blameworthy). It is a general principle of English criminal law that liability depends upon proof of conduct (*actus reus*) and a guilty mind (*mens*

The proscribed behaviour conduct or act contained within the definition of the offence. The *actus reus* of murder, for example, is the killing of a human being in the Queen's (or King's) peace (see also *Mens rea*).

Adjudication

Judgement or decision of a court or tribunal (e.g. in prison).

Adversarial

Refers to the common law justice system with a 'party prosecution' of a dispute. Parties (i.e. the Crown Prosecutor and Defence Lawyer) present the facts to the court; parties have the primary responsibility for defining the issues in a legal dispute and for investigating and advancing the dispute (not the judge – as in France or Germany). (See also Inquisitorial.)

Advocate

A barrister or solicitor representing a party in a hearing before a court (used mostly in Scotland).

AEO

Attachment of Earnings Order.

Affidavit

A written statement of evidence confirmed on oath or by affirmation to be true and taken before someone who has authority to administer it.

Affirmation

Declaration by a witness who has no religious belief, or has religious beliefs that prevent him/her taking the oath, that the evidence he is giving is the truth.

Alternative dispute resolution

(ADR) An alternative method by which parties can resolve their dispute – could be arbitration.

Annul

To declare no longer valid.

Antecedents

Information about an offender's background received in court as part of the sentencing process.

Appeal

Application to a higher court or authority for review of a decision of a lower court or authority.

Appellant	Person who appeals.
Applicant	Person making the request or demand, e.g. person who issues an application.
Application	The act of applying to a court.
Arson	See Criminal damage.
Asbo	Anti-Social Behaviour Order (civil order but criminal standards apply). *Crime and Disorder Act 1998.*
Assault	A person is guilty of assault if he intentionally or recklessly causes another person to apprehend the application of immediate and unlawful force (see *Venna* [1976] CA).
B	
Bail	Release of a defendant from custody, until his/her next appearance in court, subject sometimes to security being given and/or compliance with certain conditions.
Bailiff	Officer of the County Court empowered to serve Court documents and execute warrants.
Bankrupt	Insolvent – unable to pay creditors and having all goods/effects administered by a liquidator or trustee and sold for the benefit of those creditors; as a result of an order under the *Insolvency Act 1986.*
Bar	The collective term for barristers.
Barrister	A member of the bar – the branch of the legal profession which has rights of audience before all courts.
Basic Intent Crimes	An offence where recklessness will suffice. Offences of basic intent include:

- Involuntary manslaughter – <u>Lipman</u> (1970)
- Rape; sexual offences (*Sexual Offences Act 1956*, s 1)
- Malicious wounding; GBH (OAPA 1861, s 20) <u>Majewski</u> [1956]
- Criminal damage (*Criminal Damage Act 1971*, s 1(1)) <u>R v G</u> [2003]
- ABH (*OAPA 1861*, s 47)
- Common assault and battery (CJA 1988, s 39).

Battery

A person is guilty of battery if he intentionally or recklessly applies unlawful force to the body of another person (CJA 1988, s 39) (see *Fagan v Metropolitan Police Commissioner* [1969] 1 QB 439).

Bench warrant

A warrant issued by the judge for an absent defendant to be arrested and brought before a court by the police.

Bill of Indictment

A written statement of the charges against a defendant sent for trial to the Crown Court, and signed by an officer of the court.

Bind over

Form of sentence of unspecified date in the Magistrates' Court (rarely in the Crown Court); signed by an officer of the court. Failure to observe this order may result in a forfeit or penalty to be enforced.

Brief

Written instructions to counsel to appear at a hearing on behalf of a party prepared by the solicitor and setting out the facts of the case and any case law relied upon.

Burden of proof

In general, the prosecution must prove the defendant's guilt beyond any reasonable doubt. (See *Woolmington v DPP* [1935] HL). (See also *Insanity; Diminished responsibility*.)

C

Case	Lawsuit. Comprehensive term for any proceeding in a court, whereby an individual seeks a legal remedy (e.g. against a landlord in civil law or the crown against a defendant in criminal law).
Case law	Also known as 'common law' or 'judge made law'. Refers to judges' decisions when they try a case. Decisions are known as 'judgements'.
Case name	Each legal case in court is given a name, usually based on the family name of the parties involved e.g. *R v Smith* (R – Rex/Regina) the Crown's case against (versus) Smith.
Case number	A unique reference number allocated to each case by the issuing court.
Case to answer	The prosecution evidence must always be sufficient in itself to support a conviction or the charge must be dismissed on the ground that there is 'no case to answer'.
Caution	1. Warning, given by a Police Officer to a person charged with an offence 2. Warning, given by a Police Officer, instead of a charge.
CCRC	Criminal Cases Review Commission.
CDH	Criminal Directions Hearing. Hearing by a bench, single Magistrate or justices' clerk (or legal advisor) to deal with issues of case management.
Chambers	1. Private room, or court from which the public are excluded in which a District Judge (DJ) or Judge may conduct certain sorts of hearings 2. Offices used by a barrister.

Charge

A formal accusation against a person that a criminal offence has been committed.

CICA

Criminal Injuries Compensation Authority.

Circuit judge

A judge who sits in the County Court and/or Crown Court.

Civil

Matters concerning private rights and not offences against the state.

Civil justice reforms

The result of the Access to Justice Report by Lord Woolf (1999). The aim was to provide more effective access to justice through quicker, cheaper and more proportionate justice for defended cases. It introduced a unified set of Rules and Practice Directions for the County and High Courts, and Judicial Case Management.

CJA

Criminal Justice Act e.g. CJA 2003.

CJU

Criminal Justice Unit (e.g. of the police or the Crown Prosecution Service working jointly).

Claimant

The person issuing the claim; also known as the Plaintiff.

Committal

1. Committal for trial: Following examination by the Magistrates of a case involving an indictable or either-way offence; the procedure of directing the case to the Crown Court to be dealt with there because of seriousness
2. Committal for Sentence: Where Magistrates consider that the offence justifies a sentence greater than they are empowered to impose, they may commit the defendant to the Crown Court for sentence to be passed by a judge
3. Committal Order: An order of the Court committing someone to prison.

Common law	The law established, by precedent, from judicial decisions and established within a community (see Case law).
Community sentence	Single 'community punishment' order under CJA 2003 with a number of options attached (e.g. unpaid work in the community) available to justices instead of a prison sentence.
Compensation order	Sum of money to make up for or make amends for loss, breakage, hardship, inconvenience or personal injury caused by another (*Crime and Disorder Act 1998*).
Concurrent sentence	A direction by a court that a number of sentences of imprisonment should run at the same time.
Conditional discharge (CD)	A form of sentence: convicted defendant is discharge on condition that he does not reoffend within a specified period of time.
Consecutive sentence	An order for a subsequent sentence of imprisonment to commence as soon as a previous sentence expires; applies to two or more sentences.
Contempt of court	Disobedience or wilful disregard to the judicial process (*Contempt of Court Act 1981*).
Corroboration	Evidence by one person confirming that of another or supporting evidence, for example, forensic evidence (bloodstain, fibres etc) in murder cases.
Counsel	A barrister.
Count	An individual offence set out in an indictment.
Court of Appeal (CA)	Divided into: i) civil divisions from decisions in the High Court and Country Courts

ii) criminal divisions; hears appeals against convictions or sentences passed by the Crown Court.

Court room

The room in which cases are heard.

CPO

Community Punishment Order (now replaced by single 'Community Sentence' – CJA 2003).

CPRO

Community Punishment and Rehabilitation Order (now one option under Community Sentence).

CPS

Crown Prosecution Service.

Crime

An activity that is classified within the criminal laws of a country. Specific form of deviance; breaking of legal state norms (rules). (See also Deviance.)

Criminal

Person who has been found guilty of a criminal offence.

Criminal damage

Section 1(3) of the *Criminal Damage Act 1971* provides that a person who, without lawful excuse, destroys or damages any property belonging to another, intending to destroy or damage such property, or being reckless as to whether any such property would be destroyed or damaged, is guilty of an offence punishable on conviction on indictment with imprisonment for a maximum of ten years.
Section 1(2) provides that a person who, without lawful excuse, destroys or damages any property whether belonging to himself or another (a) intending to destroy or damage any property or being reckless as to whether any property would be destroyed or damaged, and (b) intending by the destruction or damage to endanger the life of another or being reckless as to whether the life of another would be thereby endangered, shall be guilty of an offence.

If the damage or destruction is caused by fire, the offence is charged as arson and is punishable with a maximum of imprisonment for life. (s 1(3)).

CRO

Community Rehabilitation Order (now one option under Community Sentence).

Crown Court

The Crown Court deals with all crime committed for trial by Magistrates' Courts. Cases for trial are heard before a judge and jury. The Crown Court also acts as an Appeal Court for cases heard and dealt with by the Magistrates.

The Crown Court is divided into tiers, depending on the type of work dealt with.

First tier

- Defended High Court Civil work
- All classes of offence in criminal proceedings
- Committals for sentence from the Magistrates' Court
- Appeals against convictions and sentences imposed at Magistrates' Court.

Second tier

- All classes of offence in criminal proceedings
- Committals for sentence from Magistrates' Court
- Appeals against convictions and sentences imposed at Magistrates' Court.

Third tier

- Class 4 offences only in criminal proceedings
- Committals for sentence from Magistrates' Court
- Appeals against convictions and sentences.

D

Damages	An amount of money claimed as compensation for physical/material loss, e.g. personal injury, breach of contract (ordered in a civil court).
Dark figure	Hidden and unreported crime statistic.
DCA	Department of Constitutional Affairs (replaced Lord Chancellor's Department).
DCW	Designated Case Worker from the CPS; usually not a lawyer.
Decarceration	This involves the process of removing people from institutions (e.g. prisons; mental hospitals) and sentencing the offender to a programme of community care. (See also Decarcerationist.)
Decarcerationist	Believes that prison walls should be torn down and that a criminal's punishment should be in the community (alternative sanctions).
Defendant (DEF.)	Person standing trial or appearing for sentence; the accused.
Deviance	Classical theme in Criminology that explains the causes of crime. (See also *Crime*.)
Diminished responsibility	*The Homicide Act 1957* s 2(1) provides that: 'Where a person kills or is a party to the killing of another, he shall not be convicted of murder if he was suffering from such abnormality of mind (whether arising from a condition of arrested or retarded development of mind or any inherent causes or induced by disease or injury) as substantially impaired his mental responsibility for his acts and omissions in doing or being a party to the killing'.

A successful plea of diminished responsibility reduces liability from murder to manslaughter. (s 2(3)).

Disclosure

Inspection of legal documents and evidential material; mutual exchange of evidence by prosecution and defence of all relevant information held by each party relating to the case.

Discontinuance

Notice given by the court, on instruction by the CPS, that they no longer wish to proceed with the case; CPS may reopen case at any time.

Dismissal

Notice given to the court by the CPS that the case is dismissed.

District judge

A judicial officer of the court whose duties involve hearing applications made within proceedings and final hearings subject to any limit of jurisdiction (previously known as 'Stipendiary Magistrates').

Divisional court

As well as having an original jurisdiction of their own, all three divisions of the High Court have appellate jurisdiction to hear appeals from lower Courts and tribunals. The Divisional Court of the Chancery Division deals with appeals in bankruptcy matters from the County Court. The Divisional Court of the Queen's Bench Division deals largely with certain appeals on points of law from many Courts. The Divisional Court of the Family Division deals largely with appeals from Magistrates' Courts in matrimonial matters.

Dock

Enclosure in criminal court for the defendant on trial.

DTTO

Drug Treatment and Testing Order; part of 'Community Sentence'.

E

ECHR

European Convention on Human Rights and Fundamental Freedoms (The Convention); also refers to the European Court of Human Rights in Strasbourg.

EFH

Early first hearing: The early listing before a bench of Magistrates of a straightforward case where a plea of guilty is anticipated (usually motoring offences or shoplifting). Usually dealt with (on the prosecution side) by a designated case worker (see DCW).

Either-way offence

An offence for which the accused may elect the case to be dealt with either summarily by the Magistrates or by committal to the Crown Court to be tried by jury.

Enforcement

Method of pursuing a civil action after judgement has been made in favour of a party. Process carried out by Magistrates' Court to collect fines and other monetary orders made in the Crown Court.

Estate

The rights and assets of a person in property.

Execution

Seizure of debtors' goods following non-payment of a court order.

Executor

A person or persons specified to carry out the provisions of a will.

Exempt

To be freed from liability.

Exhibit

Item or document used as evidence during a court trial.

Ex Parte

In the absence of a party to the proceedings. Usually means a one-sided application under judicial review (now 'on the application of').

Expert witness

A qualified person giving evidence on a subject in which they have expertise in a trial (e.g. a medical practitioner; forensic examiner; computer specialist). Experts can give evidence of opinion, and be given permission by the court to sit in court to hear other witnesses before they give evidence.

F

FEE

Monies payable on issue of a claim or subsequent process (e.g. a statutory declaration made in Magistrates' Court).

G

GBH

Grievous bodily harm, defined in *DPP v Smith* as meaning 'really serious harm'. GBH also includes psychological harm (see *Burstow* [1998] HL).

Going equipped

I.e. for theft or burglary, or cheat (contrary to the *Theft Act 1968*).

Guardian

A person appointed to safeguard/protect/ manage the interests of a child or person under mental disability.

H

Handling

Stolen property.

Hate crime

Group harms which are aimed at specific minority groups (e.g. homosexuals); hate crimes involve racial intimidation, ethnicity, religion, or other minority groups. Includes assaults, graffiti, property attacks.

HDC

Home Detention Curfew (also electronic tagging).

High court

A civil court which consists of three divisions:

1. Queen's Bench (can be known as King's Bench Division if a King is assuming the throne) – civil disputes for recovery of money, including breach of contract, personal injuries, libel/slander

2. Family – concerned with matrimonial matters and proceedings relating to children, e.g. wardship
3. Chancery – property matters including fraud and bankruptcy.

Homicide

There are a number of offences involving homicide. The two most important are murder and manslaughter. They share a common *actus reus* – the killing of a human being. Involuntary manslaughter differs form murder in terms of the *mens rea* required, whereas, it is the availability of one of a number of specific defences that distinguishes voluntary manslaughter form murder. (See *Provocation; Diminished responsibility; Intention.*)

Hostile witness

A witness seemingly biased against the person calling them as a witness and evading what they said in a previous, out of court, statement. If the court agrees, they can be cross-examined by the person calling them.

HRA

Human Rights Act 1998.

I

Indictable offence

A criminal offence triable only by the Crown Court. The different types of offence are classified 1, 2, 3 or 4. Murder is a class 1 offence.

In camera

In private. Exceptionally, the public and usually press, can be excluded and Magistrates can sit in private. Usually in youth or family courts.

Injunction

An order by a court either restraining a person or persons from carrying out a course of action or directing a course of action be complied with. Failure to carry out terms of the order may be punishable by imprisonment.

Inquisitorial

Refers to civil code justice systems (e.g. Germany; France; Spain; Greece) in which the 'inquisitorial' judge has primary responsibility to investigate the case.

Insanity

As the defence of insanity concerns the effect of psychological conditions upon responsibility, the question whether a defendant can take advantage of the defence is a legal question and is not resolved simply by reference to the medical evidence. The legal definition of insanity is contained in the *M'Naghten Rules* (1843):

1. Everyone is presumed sane until the contrary is proved
2. It is a defence for the defendant to prove that he was labouring under a defect of reason, due to disease of the mind, such that he either did not know the nature and quality of his act or, if he did know that, he did not know that what he was doing was wrong.

Intention (*mens rea*)

The *mens rea* for a number of offences is defined in terms of 'intention' or 'with intent to...', or 'intentionally' etc. indicating that recklessness will not suffice. Where it is not the defendant's aim or purpose but he foresaw that it was a virtually certain result of his actions then the jury may infer that he intended it. (See *Moloney* [1985] HL; *Hancock and Shankland* [1986] HL; *Nedrick* [1986] CA; *Savage and Parmenter* [1991] HL).

Intoxication

Although a lack of *mens rea* caused by voluntary intoxication will 'excuse' a crime of 'specific intent', the defendant may be convicted of an offence of 'basic intent' despite his lack of *mens rea*. (See *Majewski* [1987] HL; *Lipman* [1970]).

J

JSB

Judicial Studies Board; body which advises Lord Chancellor on the training of Magistrates.

Judge	An officer appointed to administer the law and who has authority to hear and try cases in a court of law.
Judgement	Final decision of a court.
Judicial/Judiciary	1. Relating to the administration of justice or to the judgement of a court 2. A judge or other officer empowered to act as a judge.
Jurisdiction	The area and matters over which a court has legal authority.
Juror	(See *Jury*) A person who has been summoned by a court to be a member of the jury.
Jury	Body of jurors sworn to reach a verdict according to the evidence in a Crown Court (or High Court in defamation (e.g. libel) actions; also in an inquest).
Justice of the Peace (JP)	A lay Magistrate. Member of the public appointed to administer judicial business in a Magistrates' Court; unpaid and usually not a lawyer. Also sits in the Crown Court with a judge or recorder to hear appeals and committals for sentence.
Juvenile	Person under 18 years of age.

L

Law	The system made up of rules established by an act of parliament, custom or practice enjoining or prohibiting certain action. (See also *Common law.*)
Law Lords	Describes the judges of the House of Lords who are known as the Lords of Appeal in Ordinary.

Law reports	'Test' cases that lay down important legal principles. Over 2000 law reports published each year (e.g. 'All England Law Reports' – All ER). Each case is given a reference to explain where exactly it can be found (i.e. year, volume e.g. criminal appeal reports: Cr App R. or Queen's Bench Division: QBD and page number).
Limited right	Right by virtue of the HRA (see *HRA*) – so that, within the scope of the limitation, the infringement of a guaranteed right may not contravene the Convention.
Listing questionnaire	This form is used to ensure that all issues are resolved and that the parties are ready for trial. Used for Fast Track and Multi Track claims only.
Litigation	Legal proceedings.
Lord Chancellor	Cabinet minister who acts as Speaker of the House of Lords and oversees the hearings of the Law Lords. Responsibilities include supervising the procedure of courts other than Magistrates' or Coroners Courts and selection of judges, Magistrates, Queen's counsel and members of tribunals (see *DCA*).
Lord chief justice	Senior judge of the Court of Appeal (Criminal Division) who also heads the Queen's Bench Division of the High Court of Justice.
Lord justice of appeal	Title given to certain judges sitting in the Court of Appeal.

M

Magistrate	Or Justice of the Peace (JP) – carries out legal duties in the local criminal court (see *Magistrates' Court*). JPs are unpaid and lay persons (not legally qualified); they deal with most criminal cases in less serious offences (summary

and triable-either-way e.g. minor theft, criminal damage, public disorder and motoring offences). When sitting in the Family Proceedings Court they deal with a range of issues affecting families and children, and on special committees they deal with gaming and betting shop applications.

Magistrates' Court

A court where criminal proceedings are commenced before Justices of the Peace who examine the evidence/statements and either deal with the case themselves or commit to the Crown Court for trial or sentence. Also has jurisdiction in a range of civil matters (e.g. family court).

Malice aforethought

A misleading term, signifying the *mens rea* for murder, i.e. an intention to kill or cause grievous bodily harm (see *GBH*).

Malicious wounding

Inflicting grievous bodily harm (see GBH) –.an offence under s 20 OAPA 1861, punishable with a term of imprisonment not exceeding five years. GBH can include very serious psychological harm (see *Ireland and Burstow* [1998] HL).

Manslaughter

There are several modes of committing manslaughter:

1. *Constructive manslaughter.* Also known as 'killing by an unlawful act', this offence is committed where the defendant *intentionally* commits an unlawful and dangerous act resulting in death.

2. *'Reckless' manslaughter* requires *Caldwell*-type recklessness with respect to some injury.

3. *Provocation – manslaughter.* A person (the defendant), who killed with malice aforethought will, nevertheless, be acquitted of murder and convicted of manslaughter if, at the time of the killing, the defendant, as

result of *provocation*, suffered a sudden and temporary loss of self – control and the jury are satisfied that the reasonable man would, in the circumstances, have done as the defendant did.

4. *Diminished responsibility – manslaughter.* If the defendant killed with malice afore-thought but was, at the relevant time, suf-fering from diminished responsibility, then s/he will be convicted of manslaughter (see *Ahluwalia* [1993]).

Master of the Rolls (MR)   Senior judge of the Court of Appeal (Civil Division).

MCA   Magistrates' Courts Act 1980.

McKenzie friend   Unqualified person who can be allowed by the court to assist a defendant informally. The name 'McKenzie friend' technically disap-peared after a Leicester community charge case; although it is often still used. The defen-dant has a right to such assistance unless there are compelling reasons to disallow it.

Mens rea   The term refers to the state of mind expressly or impliedly required by the definition of the offence charged. Most serious (and certain lesser) crimes require the prosecutor to estab-lish some mental element, e.g. an intention to or recklessness concerning an assault or crim-inal damage. (see *actus reus*). In the case of murder, the prosecution must prove that the defendant intended to kill or cause some seri-ous harm.

Minor   Someone below 18 years of age and unable to sue or be sued without representation, other than for wages. A minor sues by a next friend and defends by a guardian.

Mitigation   Reasons submitted on behalf of a guilty party in order to excuse or partly excuse the offence com-mitted in an attempt to minimise the sentence.

Murder

Murder is committed where the defendant, *intending* to kill or cause grievous bodily harm (*GBH*), caused the death of a human being. The offence carries a mandatory penalty of imprisonment for life (life imprisonment – life sentence).

N

Newton hearing

A 'trial within a trial' to determine the facts in the event of dispute following a 'guilty' plea (e.g. the amount stolen; were injuries caused by fists or feet?).

Next friend

(See *Guardian.*) A person representing a minor or mental patient who is involved in legal proceedings.

NOMS

National Offender Management Service; new Government agency since 2004 'joining up' Prison and Probation Services.

Non-molestation

An order within an injunction to prevent one person physically attacking another.

NPS

National Probation Service.

O

OASys

Offender Assessment System used by the NPS in Pre-Sentence Reports and offenders' risk assessment.

Oath

(See *Affirmation.*) A verbal promise by a person with religious beliefs to tell the truth.

Official solicitor

A solicitor or barrister appointed by the Lord Chancellor and working in the Lord Chancellor's Department. The duties include representing, in legal proceedings, people who are incapable of looking after their own affairs i.e. children/persons suffering from mental illness.

Omission	Apart from those offences defined specifically in terms of an 'omission to act', English law imposes liability for omissions only where it can be said that the defendant was under a duty to act. There is no general obligation to act for the benefit of others. The duty to act to save or preserve the life of another arises only in a number of stereotyped situations (e.g. parental duty; doctor's duty; see <u>Airdale NHS Trust v Bland</u> [1993] HL).
Oral examination	A method of questioning a person under oath before an officer of the court to obtain details of their financial affairs.
Original offence	Where an offender breaches certain court orders (e.g. Community Sentence; CD etc) they can be dealt with for the original offence as well as for any new offence.
Order	A direction by a court.
P	
Party	Any of the participants in a court action or proceedings.
Penal notice	Directions attached to an order of a court stating the penalty for disobedience may result in imprisonment.
Personal application	Application made to the court without legal representation.
Plea	A defendant's reply to a charge put to him by a court; i.e. guilty or not guilty.
Power of arrest	An order attached to some injunctions to allow the police to arrest a person who has broken the terms of the order.
Precedent	The decision of a case which established principles of law that act as an authority for future cases of a similar nature.

Pre-Trial Review (PTR)   A preliminary appointment at which the Magistrates or District Judge consider the issues before the court and fix the timetable for the trial.

Prosecution   (See also CPS.) The institution or conduct of criminal proceedings against a person.

Prosecutor   Person who prosecutes (see *Prosecution; CPS*).

Provocation   A common law defence, amended by s 3 of the *Homicide Act 1957*. It is a defence to murder only and applies where the defendant killed the victim with *malice aforethought* but acted under a sudden and temporary loss of self- control (see *Malice aforethought*).

PSR   Pre-Sentence Report produced by the Probation Service.

Q

Qualified right   Right by virtue of the HRA (see HRA) so that in certain circumstances and under certain condi- tions, it can be interfered with.

Quash   To annul; i.e. to declare a sentence no longer valid.

Queen's bench division   See *High Court*.

Queen's Counsel (QC)   Barristers of at least ten years standing may apply to become Queen's Counsel. QCs under- take work of an important nature and are referred to as 'silks', derived from the court gown that is worn. Will be known as King's Counsel if a king assumes the throne.

R

Race   Process of social construction and a social role model through the various means of socialisa- tion (i.e. family, school, peers etc). Racial clas- sifications, a process of labelling over time outside of the family.

Recklessness

For most offences recklessness as to whether a particular consequence will result from the defendant's actions or as to whether a particular circumstance exists, will suffice for liability. For certain crimes, recklessness bears a broader meaning. This used to be determined by the *Caldwell*-type (objective) recklessness and has now been superseded by the ruling in R v G [2003] HL. Therefore, the 'reasonable person test' will now no longer apply. Now for criminal damage (including arson) *Cunningham*-type (subjective) recklessness applies which imposes on the prosecution the burden of proving that the defendant him/herself was aware of the particular risk of the consequence occurring or the circumstance existing (see: *Caldwell* [1982] HL; *Cunningham* [1957]).

Recorder

Member of the legal profession (barristers or solicitors) who are appointed to act in a judicial capacity.

Registrar

(See *District Judge*.) Registrars and deputy registrars were renamed District Judges and Deputy District Judges respectively in the *Courts and Legal Services Act 1990.*

Remand

To order an accused person to be kept in custody or placed on bail pending further court appearance.

Reparation order

An object of sentencing (and a form of sentence operating only in the youth court) i.e. reparation to a victim. The term is also used more generally to mean 'making good' by a defendant and may feature in mitigation. It is also a statutory basis for deferment of sentence (*Crime and Disorder Act 1998*).

Reprimand

Whereas an adult may be cautioned, a juvenile who admits an offence, may be reprimanded or warned by the police under a statutory scheme, instead of being prosecuted.

Restorative justice (RJ)	Form of Criminal Justice that seeks to 'repair' harm as between offenders and victims (see *Crime and Disorder Act 1998*).
Right of audience	Entitlement to appear before a court in a legal capacity and conduct proceedings on behalf of a party to the proceedings (e.g. solicitor).

S

Security	Deposit (see Surety) – or other item of value left with the court on grant of bail.
Sex offender register	Local record maintained by the police for which certain sex offenders are obliged to provide information about themselves and their whereabouts.
SI	Statutory Instrument. Rules or regulations made by a minister of state acting under an Act of Parliament. Also called 'delegated legislation' or 'Secondary Legislation'.
Silk	(See *Queen's Counsel.*) A senior barrister sometimes referred to as a leader or leading counsel.
Slander	Spoken words which have a damaging effect on a person's reputation.
Solicitor	Member of the legal profession chiefly concerned with advising clients and preparing their cases and representing them in some courts. May also act as advocates before certain courts or tribunals; not generally in Crown Courts.
Specific intent crimes	An offence of specific intent is one for which the prosecution must prove intention with respect to one or more of the elements in the *actus reus*. Recklessness will not suffice (see

Basic intent crimes). The significance of the distinction between offences of specific intent and basic intent is that whereas a lack of *mens rea* resulting from voluntary intoxication will excuse in the case of an offence of specific intent it will not excuse for crimes of basic intent. Specific intent crimes include:

- Murder (*Beard* [1920])
- GBH with intent (s 18 OAPA 1861; *Bratty* [1963])
- Theft (s 1 Theft Act 1968; *Majewski [1987]*)
- Burglary with intent to steal (s 9 *Theft Act 1968*; *Durante* [1972]).

SSR
Specific Sentence Report. A focused form of PSR (see PSR). Usually done 'on the spot' in court by the Probation Service (NPS).

Statement
A written account by a witness of the facts or details of a matter.

Statutory Instrument (SI)
A document issued by the delegated authority (usually a Government minister or committee) named within an Act of Parliament which affects the workings of the original Act, e.g. The *Prison Rules 1999* confers authority on prison governors to make rules relating to the operation of prisons under the *Prison Act 1952*).

Stay of execution
An order following which judgement cannot be enforced without leave of the court.

Strict liability
Not all offences require proof of *mens rea*. By a crime of strict liability is meant an offence of which a person may be convicted without proof of intention (*mens rea*), recklessness or even negligence. The prosecution are only obliged to prove the commission of the *actus reus* and the absence of any recognised defence (see *Adomako* [1998]).

Subpoena	A summons issued to a person directing their attendance in court to give evidence.
Summary offence	(See *Indictable; Either-way offence*) A criminal offence which is triable only by a Magistrates' Court.
Summing-up	A review of the evidence and directions as to the law by a judge immediately before a jury retires to consider its verdict.
Summons	Order to appear or to produce evidence to a court.
Summons (Jury)	Order to attend for jury service.
Summons (witness)	Order to appear as a witness at a hearing.
Supreme court of judicature	Collective name for: High Court of Justice; Crown Court; Court of Appeal.
Surety	A person's 'stands surety' i.e. gives an undertaking to be liable for another's default or non-attendance at court.
Suspended sentence	A custodial sentence which will not take effect unless there is a subsequent offence within a specified period.
T	
Tagging	Electronic tagging/monitoring (see *Home detention curfew*).
Tort	A civil wrong committed against a person for which compensation may be sought through a civil court (e.g. personal injury; neighbourhood nuisance; libel etc).
Trial window	A period of time within which the case must be listed for trial.

Tribunal	A group of people consisting of a chairman (normally solicitor/barrister) and others who exercise a judicial function to determine matters related to specific interests (e.g. Employment Tribunal).
TWC/TWOC/TWOCKING	Taking a conveyance without consent (usually a motor vehicle).

V

Verdict	The finding of guilty or not guilty by a jury.
Victim	The victim of an offence, sometimes called the aggrieved.

W

Ward of court	The title given to a minor who is the subject of a wardship order. The order ensures that custody of the minor is held by the court with day-to-day care of the minor being carried out by an individual(s) or local authority. As long as the minor remains a ward of court, all decisions regarding the minors upbringing must be approved by the court, e.g. transfer to a different school, medical treatment etc.
Wardship	High Court action making a minor a ward of court.
Warning	'Final Warning' under the statutory scheme of reprimands and warnings for juveniles only.
Warrant of committal	Method of enforcing an order of the court whereby the penalty for failing to comply with its terms is imprisonment.
Warrant of delivery	Method of enforcing a judgement for the return of goods (or value of the goods) whereby a bailiff is authorised to recover the goods (or their value) from the debtor and return them to the creditor.

Warrant of execution	Method of enforcing a judgement for a sum of money whereby a bailiff is authorised, in lieu of payment, to seize and remove goods belonging to a defendant for sale at public auction.
Warrant of possession	Method of enforcing a judgement for possession of a property whereby a bailiff is authorised to evict people and secure against re-entry.
Warrant of restitution	A remedy available following illegal re-entry of premises by persons evicted under a warrant of possession. The bailiff is authorised to evict all occupants found on the premises and re-deliver the premises to the plaintiff.
Witness	A person who gives evidence in court.
Wounding or malicious wounding with intent	(See GBH) Wounding i.e. causing grievous bodily harm *with intent* (*mens rea* – see *Belfon* [1976] CA; *Bryson* [1985] CA; *Purcell* [1986] CA). An offence under s 18 *OAPA* 1861. The maximum penalty is a term of imprisonment for life (life sentence). To amount to a 'wound' the inner and outer skin must be broken; a bruise is not a wound ('a break in the continuity of the whole of the skin; a 'rapture of an internal blood vessel'; see *JCC (a minor) v Eisenhower* [1984] QB). Breaking a collarbone is not 'wounding' under s 18, but amounts to GBH s 20 OAPA 1861 (see *Wood* [1830]).

Y

YOI	Young Offender Institution (prison for young offenders, usually under 18, at times up to 21).
Youth justice Board	Government agency dealing with young and juvenile offenders.
YOT	Youth Offending Team. Inter-agency dealing with reports on and community sentences for juveniles.

4.3

bibliography

Allan, G. (1985) *Family Life: Domestic Roles and Social Organisation*. Oxford: Basil Blackwell.

Ashworth, A. (2003) *Principles of Criminal Law*. 4th ed. Oxford: Oxford University Press (OUP).

Ashworth, A. and Redmayne, M. (2005) *The Criminal Process*. 3rd ed. Oxford: OUP.

Back, L. (1996) *New Ethnicities and Urban Multiculture: racisms and multiculture in young lives*. London: UCL Press.

Bean, P. and Nemitz, T. (2004) *Drug Treatment: what works?* London: Routledge.

Bentham, J. (1789; 1948 edition by W. Harrison) *Introduction to the Principles of Morals and Legislation*. New York: Free Press.

Billingsley, R., Nemitz, T. and Bean, P. (eds) (2001) *Informers: policing, policy, practice*. Cullompton, Devon: Willan.

Blackstone's Statutes on Criminal Law (edited by P.R. Glazebrook) (2004) 14th ed. London: Blackstones.

Bottoms, A. (1990) 'The aims of imprisonment', in Garland, D. (ed.) *Justice, Guilt and Forgiveness in the Penal System*. Edinburgh: University of Edinburgh.

Bowlby, J. (1988) *Secure Base*. London: Penguin.

Bowlby, J. (1979) *The Making and Breaking of Affectional Bonds*. London/Baltimore: Harmondsworth-Penguin.

Bowlby, J. (1944) 'Forty-four juvenile thieves', in *International Journal of Psychology, 25*, pp. 1–75.

Bowling, B. and Foster, J. (2002) 'Policing and the Police', in Maguire, M., Morgan, R. and Reiner, R. (eds) (2002) *The Oxford Handbook of Criminology*. 3rd ed. Oxford: OUP. Chapter 27, pp. 980–1033.

Bowling, B. and Phillips, C. (2002) *Racism, Crime and Justice*. London: Longman.

Brogden, M. and Preeti, N. (2000) *Crime, Abuse and the Elderly*. Cullompton: Willan.

Brown, A. (2003) *English Society and the Prisons: time, culture and politics in the development of the modern prison 1850–1920*. London: Boydell Press.

Brown, S. and Macmillan, J. (1998) *Understanding Youth and Crime: listening to youth?* Oxford: OUP.

Brownlee, I. (1998) *Community Punishment: A Critical Introduction*. London: Longman.

Campbell, A. (1981) *Girl Delinquents*. Oxford: Blackwell.

Carlen, P. (ed.) (2002) *Women and Punishment: the struggle for justice*. Cullompton: Willan.

Carlen, P. and Worrall, A. (2004) *Analysing Women's Imprisonment.* Cullompton: Willan.

Carter, P. (2003) *Managing Offenders, Reducing Crime: a new approach (The Carter Report).* London. Cabinet Office Strategy Unit.

Cavadino, M. and Dignan, J. (2001) *The Penal System.* 2nd ed. London: Sage.

Cohen, S. (1972) *Folk Devils and Moral Panics: the creation of the Mods and Rockers.* London: Macgibbon and Kee.

Corrigan, P. (1979) *Schooling the Smash Street Kids.* London: Macmillan.

Croall, H. (2001) *Understanding White Collar Crime.* Oxford: OUP.

Crown Prosecution Service (2003) *Race for Justice: A Review of the Crown Prosecution Service Decision Making for Possible Racial Bias at each Stage of the Prosecution Process.* London: CPS.

Davies, M., Croall, H. and Tyrer, J. (2005) *An Introduction to the Criminal Justice System of England and Wales.* 3rd ed. London: Pearson/Longman.

Downes, D. and Rock, P. (2003) *Understanding Deviance.* 4th ed. Oxford: OUP.

Durkheim, E. (1893; 1933) *The Division of Labour in Society* (trans. George Simpson). Glencoe, IL: Free Press.

Durkheim, E. (1897) *Suicide: A study of sociology.* New York: Free Press.

Easton, S. and Piper, C. (2005) *Sentencing and Punishment: the quest for justice.* Oxford: OUP.

Elliott, C. and Quinn, F. (2005) *English Legal System.* 5th ed. London: Longman/Pearson.

Elliot, F.R. (1996) *Gender, Family, and Society.* Basingstoke: Macmillan.

Emsley, C. (2004) *Crime and Society in England: 1750–1900.* 3rd ed. Harlow, Essex: Longman.

Farrington, D., Barnes, G. and Lambert, S. (1996) 'The concentration of offending in families', in *Legal and Criminological Psychology 1*, pp. 47–63.

Fattah, E.A. and Sacco, V.F. (1989) *Crime and Victimization of the Elderly.* New York and Berlin: Springer Verlag.

Faulkner, D. (2001) *Crime, State and Citizen: a field full of folk.* Winchester: Waterside Press.

Ferraro, K. (1995) *Fear of Crime: interpreting victimization risk.* New York: State University of New York Press.

Fitzgerald, M., Stockdale, J. and Hale, C. (2003) *Young People and Street Crime.* London: The Youth Justice Board.

Fleisher, M. (1989) *Warehousing Violence* (part of the 'Frontiers of Anthropology Series – Vol 3) Newbury Park, California and London: Sage.

Foucault, M. (1975) *Discipline and Punish: the birth of the prison.* London: Allen Lane.

Garland, D. (1990) *Punishment and Modern Society: a study in social theory.* Oxford: Clarendon.

Gibson, B. and Watkins, M. (2004) *The Criminal Justice Act 2003: a guide to the new procedures and sentencing.* Winchester: Waterside Press.

Gladstone, Sir William E. (1895) *Report of the Home Office Committee on Prisons (The Gladstone Report)*. London.

Glueck, S. and Glueck, E.T. (1950) *Unravelling Juvenile Delinquency*. Cambridge, MA: Harvard University Press.

Gobert, J. and Punch, M. (2003) *Rethinking Corporate Crime*. London: Butterworths/LexisNexis.

Goldson, B. (ed.) (2000) *The New Youth Justice*. Russell House.

Grove, T. (2003) *The Magistrate's Tale: a front line report from a new JP*. London: Bloomsbury.

Hale, C., Hayward, K., Wahidin, A. and Wincup, E. (eds) (2005) *Criminology*. Oxford: OUP.

Hall, S. and Jefferson, T. (eds) (1976) *Resistance Through Rituals: youth subcultures in post-war Britain*. London: Unwin Hyman.

Heaton, R. (2004) *Criminal Law*. Oxford: OUP.

Herring, J. (2005) *Criminal Law: text, cases, and materials*. Oxford: OUP.

Hirschi, T. (1969) *Causes of Delinquency*. London: Sage.

Hopkins Burke, R. (ed.) (2004) *Hard Cop, Soft Cop: dilemmas and debates in contemporary policing*. Cullompton: Willan.

Hough, M. (1987) 'Thinking About Effectiveness', *British Journal of Criminology, 27(1)*, pp. 70; 73.

Hough, M. and Mayhew, P. (1983) *Taking Account of Crime: key findings from the 1984 British Crime Survey*. Home Office Research Study No. 85. London: HMSO.

Howard, J. (1777) *The State of the Prisons in England and Wales*. Reprint edition by R.W. England JR (1973) Montclair, New Jersey: Patterson Smith Publishers.

Hoyle, C. (ed.) (2002) *New Visions of Crime Victims*. London: Hart.

Hughes, G. (2001) 'The Competing Logics of Community Sanctions: Welfare, Rehabilitation and Restorative Justice', in McLaughlin, E. and Muncie, J. (eds) *Controlling Crime*. 2nd ed. London: Sage.

Hungerford-Welch, P. (2004) *Criminal Litigation and Sentencing*. 6th ed. London: Cavendish.

James, A. and Raine, J. (1998) *The New Politics of Criminal Justice*. London: Longman.

James, E. (2003) *A Life Inside: a prisoner's notebook*. Atlantic Books.

Jennings, D. (2003) One Year Juvenile Reconviction Rates: First Quarter of 2001 Cohort, Home Office. Report 18/03. London: Home Office.

Johnston, L. (2000) *Policing Britain: risk, security and governance*. London: Longman.

Kant, I. (1785; reprint 1993) *Die Metaphysik der Sitten* (Grounding for Metaphysics of Morals) (trans. James W. Ellington) Indianapolis: Hackett.

Kant, I. (1781; reprint 2002) *Kritik der reinen Vernunft* (The Critique of Pure Reason) (trans. Werner S. Pluhar) Indianapolis: Hackett.

Keith, M. (1993) *Race, Riots and Policing*. London: UCL Press.

Kennedy, H. (1993) *Eve Was Framed*. London: Vintage.

Leishman, F., Loveday, B. and Savage, S. (eds) (2000) *Core Issues in Policing*. London: Longman.

Liebling, A. (1992) *Suicides in Prison*. London: Routledge.

Logan, A. (1994) 'In the Name of the Father', 144 New Law Journal 294.

Longford, Lord (1991) *Punishment and the Punished*. London: Chapmans.

Mansfield, M. (1993) *Presumed Guilty*. London: Heinemann.

Marsh, I. (2004) *Criminal Justice: an introduction to philosophies, theories and practice*. London: Routledge.

Martin, J. and Turner, C. (2005) *Unlocking Criminal Law*. Abingdon, Oxon: Hodder and Stoughton.

Marx, K. and Engels, F. (1848) *The Communist Manifesto*. London: Harmondsworth/Penguin.

Matravers, A. (2003) *Sex Offenders in the Community: managing and reducing risk*. Cullompton: Willan.

May Report (1993) Sir John May: *Report of the inquiry into the circumstances surrounding the convictions arising out of the bomb attacks in Guildford and Woolwich in 1974*. Final Report. HC 449, para.1.12.

McColgan, A. (2000) *Women under the Law: the false promise of human rights*. London: Longman.

McConville, S. (ed.) (2003) *The Use of Punishment*. Cullompton: Willan.

McIlroy, D. (2003) *Studying at University: how to be a successful student*. London: Sage.

McLaughlin, E. (2001) 'Key Issues in Policework', in McLaughlin, E. and Muncie, J. (eds) (2001) *Controlling Crime*. 2nd ed. London: Sage. Chapter 2.

McLaughlin, E., Fergusson, R., Hughes, G. and Westmarland, L. (eds) (2003) *Restorative Justice: critical issues*. London: Sage/The Open University.

McLaughlin, E. and Muncie, J. (eds) (2006) *The Sage Dictionary of Criminology*, 2nd edn. London: Sage.

Merton, R.K. (1968) 'Social Structure and Anomie', in *Social Theory and Social Structure*. New York: Free Press, pp. 185–214.

Miller, J.G. (1992) *Last one over the Wall: The Massachusetts experiment in closing reform schools*. Ohio State University Press.

Mitchell, B. and Farrar, S. (2005) *Blackstone's Statutes on Criminal Justice and Sentencing*. 2nd ed. Oxford: OUP.

Morris, N. and Rothman, D.J. (eds) (1995) *The Oxford History of the Prison*. Oxford: OUP.

Muncie, J. (2004) *Youth and Crime*. 2nd ed. London: Sage.

Muncie, J. (2001) 'Prisons, Punishment and Penalty', in McLaughlin, E. and Muncie, J. (eds) (2001) *Controlling Crime*. 2nd ed. London: Sage.

Muncie, J. and McLaughlin, E. (2001) 'Crime, Order and Social Control', in *The Problem of Crime* – series. London: Sage.

Murray, C. (1984) *Losing Ground: American social policy 1950–1980*. London: Basic Books.

Newburn, T. (2003) *A Handbook of Policing*. Cullompton: Willan.

Newburn, T. and Stanko, E. (eds) (1994) *Just Boys Doing Business?* London: Routledge.

Parsons, T. and Bales, R. (1956) *Family, Socialisation and Interaction Process*. London: Routledge and Kegan Paul.

Peckham, A. (1985) *A Woman in Custody: a personal account of one nightmare journey through the English penal system*. London: Fontana.

Prison Service Order 4950 (1999) *Regimes for under 18 year olds*. London: HM Prison Service.

Punch, M. (1985) *Conduct Unbecoming: the social construction of police deviance and control*. London: Tavistock.

Radzinowicz, L. and Wolfgang, M. (eds) (1977) *The Criminal under Restraint*. 2nd ed. in Crime and Justice. Vol 3. New York/London: Basic Books.

Ramsbotham, Sir David (former Chief Inspector of Prisons) (2003) *Prisongate: The shocking state of Britain's prisons and the need for visionary change*. London: Simon and Schuster.

Rawlings, P. (1999) *Crime and Power: a history of criminal justice 1688–1998*. London: Longman.

Rawls, J. (1971; 1999 reprinted edition) *A Theory of Justice*. Oxford: OUP.

Raynor, P. (2002) 'Community Penalties: Probation, Punishment, and "What Works"', in Maguire, M., Morgan, R. and Reiner, R. (eds) *The Oxford Handbook of Criminology*. 3rd ed. Oxford: OUP. Chapter 31, pp. 1168–96.

Rebellon, C.J. (2002) 'Reconsidering the Broken Homes – Delinquency Relationship and Exploring its Mediating Mechanims(s)', *Criminology*, 40(1), pp. 103–36.

Rehman, J. (2003) *International Human Rights Law: a practical approach*. London: Longman.

Reiner, R. (2000) *The Politics of the Police*. 3rd ed. Oxford: OUP.

Reynolds, J. and Smartt, U. (eds) (1996) *Prison Policy and Practice*. HMP Leyhill: HM Prison Service.

Roberts, J. and Hough, M. (2002) *Changing Attitudes to Punishment: public opinion, crime and justice*. Cullompton: Willan.

Rowe, M. (2004) *Policing, Race and Racism*. Cullompton: Willan.

Runciman, W.G. (1996) *Relative Deprivation and Social Justice: a study of attitudes to social inequality in 20th century England*. London: Routledge and Kegan Paul.

Saraga, E. (2001) 'Dangerous Places: The Family as a Site of Crime', in Muncie, J. and McLaughlin, E. (eds) *The Problem of Crime*. 2nd ed. London: Sage. Chapter 5.

Sereny, G. (1998) *Cries Unhead: The story of Mary Bell*. London: Macmillan.

Scrivener, A. (1989) 'The Guildford Four', *Counsel*, November, p. 15.

Sewell, T. (1997) *Black Masculinities and Schooling: how black boys survive modern schooling*. Staffordshire: Trentham.

Slapper, G. and Kelly, D. (2004) *The English Legal System*. 7th ed. London: Cavendish.

Smartt, U. (2001/02) 'The Stalking Phenomenon: Trends in European and International Stalking and Harassment Legislation', *European Journal of Crime, Criminal Law and Criminal Justice*, Vol 9/3, pp. 209–32.

Smartt, U. (2001) *Grendon Tales: stories from a therapeutic community*. Winchester: Waterside Press.

Social Exclusion Unit (2002) *Reducing Re-Offending by Ex-Prisoners*. London: TSO.

Sullivan, D. and Tifft, L. (2006) *Handbook of Restorative Justice: a global perspective*. London: Routledge.

Thrasher, F. (1963) *The Gang*. Chicago: University of Chicago Press.

Treadwell, J. (2006) *Criminology*. London: Sage.

Vanstone, M. (2004) *Supervising Offenders in the Community: a history of probation theory and practice*. Aldershot, Hants: Ashgate.

von Hirsch, A. and Ashworth, A. (2005) *Proportionate Sentencing: exploring the principles*. Oxford: OUP.

Wakefield, A. (2003) *Selling Security: the private policing of public spaces*. Cullompton: Willan.

Walker, C. and Starmer, K. (1999) *Miscarriages of Justice: A review of justice in error*. London: Blackstone Press.

Walklate, S. (2004) *Gender, Crime and Criminal Justice*. 2nd ed. Cullompton: Willan.

Walklate, S. (2001) 'Community and Crime Prevention', in McLaughlin, E. and Muncie, J. (eds) *Controlling Crime*. 2nd ed. London: Sage.

Whitfield, D. (2001) *An Introduction to the Probation Service*. 2nd ed. Winchester. Waterside Press.

Williams, K.S. (2004) *Textbook on Criminology*. 5th ed. Oxford: OUP.

Wilson, D., Ashton, J. and Sharp, D. (2001) *What Everyone in Britain should know about the Police*. London: Blackstone.

Worrall, A. and Hoy, C. (eds) (2005) *Punishment in the Community: making offenders, making choices*. Cullompton: Willan.

Wyner, R. (2003) *From the Inside: life in a women's prison – By a charity worker who should never have been there*. London: Aurum Press.

Zander, M. (2001) 'Should the legal profession be shaking in its boots?', *New Law Journal*, 369.

Zander, M. (1999) *The Law Making Process*. London: Butterworths.

Zander, M. (1988) *A Matter of Justice*. Oxford: OUP.

Zimring, F.E. and Hawkins, G. (1995) *Incapacitation: penal confinement and the restraint of crime*. Oxford/New York: OUP.

4.4

internet sources and useful websites

Acts of Parliament: www.opsi.gov.uk/acts.htm

The Auld Report 2001 – Review of the Criminal Courts in England & Wales: www.criminal-courts-review.org.uk

Black Police Association: www.nationalbpa.com

British Crime Survey (BCS): www.homeoffice.gov.uk/rds/index.htm

British Transport Police: http://www.btp.police.uk

Commission for Racial Equality and Racism: www.cre.gov.uk

Criminal Justice System of England and Wales: www.cjsonline.gov.uk

Crown Prosecution Service (CPS): www.cps.gov.uk

Death Penalty: www.deathpenalty.org

Department for Constitutional Affairs (DCA): www.dca.gov.uk

DCA & Magistrates: www.dca.gov.uk/magistrates.htm

Her Majesty's Court Service: www.hmcourts-service.gov.uk

HM Inspectorate of Prisons: http://inspectorates.homeoffice.gov.uk/hmiprisons

HM Inspectorate of Probation: http://inspectorates.homeoffice.gov.uk/hmiprobation

HM Prison Service: www.hmprisonservice.gov.uk

Home Office: www.homeoffice.gov.uk

Howard League for Penal Reform: www.howardleague.org.uk

Identity Fraud (CIFAS): www.identityfraud.org.uk

Independent Police Complaints Commission: www.ipcc.gov.uk

International Crime Victim Survey (ICVS): www.unicri.it/wwd/analysis/icvs/index.php

Judicial Studies Board: www.jsboard.co.uk

Jury Service: www.hmcourts-service.gov.uk/infoabout/jury_service/index.htm

Law Society of England/Wales: www.lawsociety.org.uk/home.law

Legal Services Commission (CLS) (formerly 'legal aid'): www.clsdirect.org.uk/index.jsp

Local Criminal Justice Boards (42): www.lcjb.cjsonline.org

London Probation Service: www.london-probation.org.uk

Magistrates' Association: www.magistrates-association.org.uk

Metropolitan Police: www.met.police.uk

Ministry of Defence (MoD): www.mod.uk/mdp

National Association of Probation Officers (NAPO): www.napo.org.uk

National Association of Youth Justice: www.nayj.org.uk

National Probation Service: www.homeoffice.gov.uk/justice/probation

National Reassurance Policing Programme (NRPP): www.reassurance-policing.co.uk

Office of National Statistics: www.statistics.gov.uk/default.asp

Penal Reform International: www.penalreform.org

Police: www.homeoffice.gov.uk/police/

Police Information Technology Organisation (PITO): www.pito.org.uk

Prison and Probation Ombudsman: www.ppo.gov.uk

Prison population statistics: www.homeoffice.gov.uk/rds/prisons1.html

Prison Reform Trust: www.prisonreformtrust.org.uk

Scottish Prison Service: www.sps.gov.uk

Sentencing: Justice & Prisons: www.homeoffice.gov.uk/justice/what-happens-at-court/sentencing/

UK Parliament: www.parliament.uk

Victim Support: www.victimsupport.org.uk

Women in Prison: www.womeninprison.org.uk

Youth Justice Board: www.youth-justice-board.gov.uk/YouthJusticeBoard

index